JESUS CHRIST
Divine Man or Son of God?

James R. Brady

UNIVERSITY
PRESS OF
AMERICA

Lanham • New York • London

Copyright © 1992 by
University Press of America®, Inc.
4720 Boston Way
Lanham, Maryland 20706

3 Henrietta Street
London WC2E 8LU England

Library of Congress Cataloging-in-Publication Data

Brady, James R., 1950-
Jesus Christ : Divine Man or Son of God? / James R. Brady.
p.   cm.
Includes bibliographical references and index.
1. Divine man (Christology)   2. Son of God.
3. Jesus Christ—Person and offices.   I. Title.
BT205.B758   1991   232'.8—dc20   91-32969 CIP

ISBN 0-8191-8481-0 (cloth : alk. paper)

™ The paper used in this publication meets the minimum requirements of
American National Standard for Information Sciences—Permanence
of Paper for Printed Library Materials, ANSI Z39.48–1984.

Preface

This book is essentially the result of the research for my doctoral dissertation. It springs from my interest in the title "Son of God," which I hold to be the most significant of Christological titles. Its use in the *theios anēr* discussion is but one of countless applications of its truth.

In a work such as this there are so many people to recognize and to thank. I am unable to list everyone who has aided me, but the following represent some of the most helpful: to Drs. Lanier Burns, Frederic Howe and Darrell Bock for their insightful reading of my dissertation; to Ken VanHorne for his help on the illustrations; to Dr. Harold Hoehner and [soon to be Dr.] David Puckett for their help on the layout, to Mark Sadley and Tom Bailey for transferring the document; and to Dallas Theological Seminary for the use of the equipment to print out this work.

Finally, but most importantly, I must thank my family. My father and mother, Jim and Norma Brady, have been a constant source of encouragement and support through the years. Their love and godly example have built in me a foundation for committing my life to serving God and others. My children, Julie, Christen and Bonnie, have been extremely patient as I worked on the book. But most of all I thank my lovely wife, Jackie, without whom there would be little or no organization in my life. Her support and love have sustained me. She is precious beyond words--a true "helper suitable for me."

J. R. B.
Garland, Texas
August, 1991

Contents

Introduction 1
    The Subject 1
    The Purpose 2
    The Method 3

**Section 1 - Examination: The Divine Man Christology
       and the Biblical Title "Son of God"** 5

Chapter 1
    An Examination of the Divine Man Christology . . . 7
        Research Prior to Bieler 9
        Ludwig Bieler's Study 15
        Rudolf Bultmann's Transference Theory 21
        Contemporary Adherents 24
        Summary of the Divine Man Christology 35

Chapter 2
    The "Son of God" Concept in the Old Testament . . . 39
        Sonship: the Various Concepts 40
        Sonship: God as Father 43
        Unique Sonship: Israel's Messiah-king 50
        Summary of the Old Testament Background 60

Chapter 3
    The "Son of God" Title in the New Testament 63
        Jesus the Son of God:
           the Unique Messiah-king 63
        Jesus the Son of God:
           the Unique Filial Relationship with God 77
        Jesus the Son of God:
           the Unique Identification with God 85
        Summary 90

Contents

Section 2 - Refutation: The "Divine Man" as Explanation for the New Testament "Son of God" 97

**Chapter 4
The "Divine Man" as Background to
New Testament Christology** 99
 Diversity in the "Divine Man" Concept 99
 The Hellenistic Influence on Judaism 106
 *The Hellenistic versus the Hebraic Concepts
 of God and Man* 113
 Summary 118

**Chapter 5
The "Divine Man" as Explanation
for the New Testament "Son of God"** 121
 The New Testament Use of the Term θεῖος 121
 The Lack of Congruity between the Two Titles 123
  The diverse cultural backgrounds of the titles 124
  The diverse applications of the titles 129

Conclusion 135

Appendix 139

Index 143

INTRODUCTION

The Subject

In the last twenty years, the "divine man" or *theios anēr* theory has grown in popularity and has permeated contemporary Christology and Gospel studies. This theory sees a Hellenistic concept as the background to the New Testament title "Son of God" as applied to Jesus.

The divine man is seen in various roles in different individuals. Sometimes he is a miracle-worker, sometimes a seer or a wise man, teacher, savior, or hero. But in each of these roles the individual clearly manifests the presence and power of divinity.

Howard Kee says that the theory "has been repeated so often that it has come to be accepted as a fact."[1] Of its impact on Markan studies, William Lane says,

> There is a general tendency in German and American scholarship to assume that a *theios anēr* Christology is inherent within the miracle tradition and records of controversy in Mark 1-8 and within the strands of the Markan passion narrative. The particular reading of the evidence and the *theios anēr* configuration recognized within the text varies, but the assumption is scarcely questioned that behind the gospel of Mark lies a Hellenistic view of Jesus which is indebted to the image of the *theios anēr* as a miracle worker.[2]

Although the theory has gained widespread acceptance in recent years, it is not a new one by any means. It stems from the history-of-religions approach to finding parallels between the New Testament and other religions of that era and geographical region. The theory was popularized by the influential writings of Rudolf Bultmann. In

---

[1]Howard C. Kee, *Jesus in History: An Approach to the Study of the Gospels* (New York: Harcourt, Brace & World, 1970), 134.

[2]William L. Lane, *"Theios Anēr* Christology and the Gospel of Mark," in *New Dimensions in New Testament Study*, ed. Richard N. Longenecker and Merrill Tenney (Grand Rapids: Zondervan Publishing House, 1974), 148-49.

2   Jesus Christ: Divine Man or Son of God?

his *Theologie des Neuen Testaments*[3] and *Die Geschichte der synoptischen Tradition*[4] Bultmann postulated that the Christological title "Son of God" was actually the culmination of two or three separate ideas in the Hellenistic world. One of those concepts was the divine man or *theios anēr*. While the other ideas which Bultmann postulated as lying behind the "Son of God" title have been refuted and have passed from the scene, the divine man theory has gained momentum.[5]

Thus, advocates of the divine man Christology assert that the New Testament writers are presenting nothing unique in their portrayal of Jesus of Nazareth. Ancient texts testify to many heroes and miracle-workers upon whom divine status was conferred because of supposed great ability. As a *theios anēr*, Jesus takes his place among several exceptional individuals spoken of in Greek literature.

The Purpose

Although the divine man Christology has gained many adherents and has grown in popularity, there has been no comprehensive critique of the theory. Several writers have offered critical comments in individual chapters of books and in journal articles, but no exhaustive critique of the magnitude of the present study has been offered.[6]

The divine man Christology makes several assumptions and is very dependent on the study of a few key authors. It is the purpose of this study to examine the divine man Christology, and to expose any inconsistencies and lack of validity. As Leonhard Goppelt says, ". . .

---

[3]Rudolf Bultmann, *Theologie des Neuen Testaments* (Tübingen: J. C. B. Mohr (Paul Siebeck), 1958), 130-32.

[4]Idem, *Die Geschichte der synoptischen Tradition* (Göttingen: Vanderhoeck & Ruprecht, 1957), 256.

[5]Otto Betz, "The Concept of the So-Called 'Divine Man' in Mark's Gospel," in *Studies in New Testament and Early Christian Literature*, ed. David Edward Aune (Leiden: E. J. Brill, 1972), 229.

[6]Cf. Otto Betz, "The Concept of the So-Called 'Divine Man' In Mark's Gospel," 229-40; Carl R. Holladay, *Theios Anēr in Hellenistic-Judaism* (Missoula, MT: Scholars Press, 1977), passim; William L. Lane, "*Theios Anēr* Christology and the Gospel of Mark," 141-61; Howard C. Kee, "Aretalogy and Gospel," *Journal of Biblical Literature* 92 (1973):402-22; Jack Dean Kingsbury, "The 'Divine Man' as the Key to Mark's Christology--the End of an Era?" *Interpretation* 35 (1981):243-57; W. L. Liefeld, "The Hellenistic 'Divine Man' and the Figure of Jesus in the Gospels," *Journal of the Evangelical Theological Society* 16 (1973):195-205; David Lenz Tiede, *The Charismatic Figure as Miracle Worker* (Missoula, MT: Scholars Press, 1972), passim.

awareness must increase that making a standard of the *theios anēr* . . . needs to be critically reviewed . . . and made more precise."[7] The present study will attempt to meet this need.

The Method

Two of the assumptions made by the advocates of the divine man Christology concern the first century conception of the Hellenistic divine man and the biblical title "Son of God." Of the first, they assume the *theios anēr* to have been a fixed and well-known image in the Hellenistic world prior to and contemporary with the Gospel accounts.[8] With reference to the biblical title "Son of God," the divine man Christology makes the assumption that the Jewish view of this title was a socio-political one and could not fit with the miracle-working Jesus as portrayed in the Gospels. Thus, behind the ascription of this title to Jesus lay not the Old Testament and the Jewish concept of "Son of God," but the Hellenistic concept of a miracle-working divine man.[9]

This study will be divided into two main sections: examination and refutation. The examination section will attempt an understanding of each of the concepts assumed by the divine man approach. The first chapter in the section will comprehensively examine the divine man Christology, while the second and third chapters will offer an extensive examination of the biblical title "Son of God."

The refutation section will also be divided into two chapters. The first chapter of the section (chapter four) critiques the theory's inconsistencies in the handling of data concerning the divine man figure. It will critically analyze the divine man Christology's assumption as to how the *theios anēr* tradition became a part of the Gospel record. The final chapter compares and contrasts the two concepts of the Hellenistic divine man and the biblical "Son of God" to determine if indeed the Hellenistic concept might possibly serve as an explanation for the biblical title "Son of God."

Citations of untranslated German works have the corresponding quotation of the reference in the Appendix as the quote appears in the German text. This will allow the reader the opportunity to see the untranslated quote.

---

[7]Leonhard Goppelt, *Theology of the New Testament*, trans. John E. Alsup (Grand Rapids: William B. Eerdmans Publishing Company, 1982), 2:70.

[8]Hans Dieter Betz, "Jesus as the Divine Man," in *Jesus and the Historian*, ed. F. Thomas Trotter (Philadelphia: The Westminster Press, 1968), 116-17.

[9]Bultmann, *Theologie des Neuen Testaments*, 1:130-32.

SECTION 1

EXAMINATION:

THE DIVINE MAN CHRISTOLOGY AND THE BIBLICAL TITLE "SON OF GOD"

This section will entail a comprehensive study of the concepts of the divine man and Son of God. The study of the divine man in chapter 1 will be comprised of an historical tracing of the development of this approach to Christology from its beginning to contemporary adherents. The Son of God title will be examined as the concept comes from the Old Testament (Chapter 2) and is then applied to Jesus Christ in the New (Chapter 3).

The results of the study in this first section will serve as a basis for comparing these two concepts in Section 2 and will provide a frame of reference for critiquing the divine man Christology.

1

An Examination of the Divine Man Christology

Before the actual examination of the divine man Christology begins, it will be necessary to establish a definition. This is best accomplished by citing one of its present adherents,

> The term "Divine Man Christology" designates a Christology that presents the earthly Jesus of Nazareth by making use of motifs from the Hellenistic concept of the Divine Man (*theios anēr*) . . . He is exceptionally gifted and extraordinary in every respect. He is in command both of a higher, revelational wisdom and of divine power (δύναμις) to do miracles. Yet he is not identical with a deity, but can be called a mixture of the human and the divine.[1]

Those who espouse a divine man Christology realize the term *theios anēr* is not to be found in the New Testament. However, they have a rationale for that,

> As far as the New Testament is concerned, the technical term *theios anēr* is not applied to Jesus. However, since the concept can utilize a variety of honorific titles, the absence of the technical term itself is no conclusive argument against the presence of the concept. It was a Hellenistic-Jewish variation of the concept that influenced primitive Christianity, so that the presentation of Jesus naturally differs from that, for example, of Apollonius of Tyana. Furthermore, we must recognize that within the New Testament itself the concept of the Divine Man Jesus has undergone far-reaching theological developments, so that even there we encounter a variety of expressions of it. They all have in common the description of Jesus of Nazareth as divine Savior. Although they presuppose his full humanity, his significance is seen in his ability to surmount what is the nor-

---

[1]Hans Dieter Betz, "Jesus as Divine Man," in *Jesus and the Historian*, ed. F. Thomas Trotter (Philadelphia: The Westminster Press, 1968), 116.

mal human condition.[2]

This theory has become increasingly popular throughout this century. It says that such a large number of miracles are ascribed to Jesus in the Gospels, not because He did them, but because of the Hellenistic idea that the divinity of an individual was proved by his miracles.[3]

A study of the development of the divine man Christology is largely a study of a history-of-religions (*religionsgeschichte*) approach. This method sought "to understand the religion of both the Old and New Testaments within the context of their historical enviornment, including the other religions of that time and region."[4] The proponents of the *Religionsgeschichte Schule* advocated extensive use of data from the comparative study of religions while reducing dogmatic consideration to a minimum.[5] In this approach, religious documents were to be understood as products of extensive development in the community.[6] Thus, as Koester puts it, "The *religionsgeschichte* approach [held that] . . . primitive Christianity was a totally syncretistic phenomenon."[7]

With this presupposition, writers such as Hugo Gressman, Wilhelm Bousset, and Johannes Weiss claimed they saw in Scripture many passages which were based on extra-biblical myth of non-Jewish origin.[8] The New Testament merely reflected the "confluence of traditions" of the era of Hellenism.[9] It was the task of the *Religionsgeschichte Schule* to isolate the tributaries that contributed to this confluence.

Students of the *Religionsgeschichte Schule* were aware of the similarities between certain aspects of the figure of Christ as portrayed in the Gospels and the Hellenistic portrayals of apotheosized figures.[10] These latter portrayals included extraordinarily gifted

---

[2]Ibid., 117.

[3]W. Nicol, The Sēmeia in the Fourth Gospel: Tradition and Redaction (Leiden: E. J. Brill, 1972), 48.

[4]Richard N. Soulen, *"Religionsgeschichte"* in *Handbook of Biblical Criticism* (Atlanta: John Knox Press, 1981), 167.

[5]*The Oxford Dictionary of the Christian Church*, s.v., "Religionsgeschichte Schule," n.a., 1171.

[6]Ibid.

[7]Helmut Koester, "The Theological Aspects of Primitive Christian Heresy," in *The Future of Our Religious Past*, 69.

[8]*The Oxford Dictionary of the Christian Church*, 1171.

[9]David Lenz Tiede, *The Charismatic Figure as Miracle Worker* (Missoula, MT: Scholars Press, 1972), 292.

[10]Walter L. Liefeld, "The Hellenistic 'Divine Man' and the Figure of Jesus in

men, miracle-workers, healers, or wise men.[11] From Homeric time onwards the Greeks regarded such individuals as more than human. They were divine or *theioi*.[12] A. D. Nock says of the term, "θεῖος is properly applicable to that which belongs to the gods or partakes of their qualities."[13] Thus, in the *Religionsgeschichte Schule* the term became linked with New Testament Christology. This chapter will trace the development of the divine man Christology from its inception, through the apex of its expression in Ludwig Bieler, its incorporation in Bultmann's "transference theory," and its major contemporary adherents. The list of writers which follows is not intended to represent everyone who can be linked with the position. However, those included have been the most influential in the development and expression of the concept.

Research Prior to Bieler

Although Ludwig Bieler asserts that he is the first to delineate extensively the ancient Greco-Roman concept of the *theios anēr*,[14] he is by no means the first to link this Hellenistic concept with the person of Jesus Christ. In fact, such comparisons between Jesus and figures in Hellenistic literature can be traced back into the nineteenth century to writers such as F. C. Baur. In his *Apollonius von Tyana und Christus*, Baur points out the similarities between the famous Hellenistic miracle worker and Jesus. These similarities, included in a section entitled "The Proof of the Parallels between Apollonius and Christ," extended to their births, their working of miracles, personal characteristics, and the sentence of death pronounced upon both.[15] Although Baur nowhere employs the term *theios* in his work, the foundation was laid for such comparisons. In fact, Apollonius is later viewed as one of the key examples of the divine man.[16]

It was not until the turn of the century, however, that the *theios*

---

the Gospels," *Journal of the Evangelical Theological Society* 16 (1973):195.

[11]Ibid.

[12]Arthur Darby Nock, *Essays on Religion and the Ancient World*, ed. by Zeph Stewart (Oxford: Clarendon Press, 1972), 1:145.

[13]Ibid., 1:367-68.

[14]Ludwig Bieler, ΘΕΙΟΣ ANHP. *Das Bild des "Göttlichen Mensch" in Spätantike und Frühchristentum* (Reprint, Darmstadt: Wissenschaftliche Buchgesellschaft, 1976), 1:4-5.

[15]Ferdinand Christian Baur, *Apollonius von Tyana und Christus. Ein Beitrag zur Religionsgeschichte der ersten Jahrhunderte nach Christus* (Reprint, Hildesheim: Georg Olms Verlagsbuchhandlung, 1966), 138-41.

[16]Bieler, 1:17.

anēr (or *theios anthrōpos*) was pointed out by name. Richard Reitzenstein provided much of the basic data used to correlate the image of Jesus in the canonical gospels with the depictions of other figures in the ancient world who were held to have attained divine status.[17] This he did in two wide-ranging studies, one of Hellenistic miracle stories and the other of Hellenistic mystery religions. The first, a 1906 work entitled *Hellenistische Wundererzahlungen*, alludes to the *theios anēr* as one who foresees his death and is abandoned by his faithful followers to die alone.[18] The second work, *Die Hellenistischen Mysterienreligion* published in 1910 spoke of the general conception of the divine man. This conception included visionary and miraculous powers and personal holiness.[19] Although Reitzenstein does not overtly link the person of Christ with the *theios anēr* concept of Hellenism in either work, a footnote in the earlier work refers to the dispute over the divine nature, the θεῖα φύσις, of Christ.[20] Reitzenstein's work intimated, furthermore, that this Hellenistic theology entered Judaism in the writings of Philo.[21] It was Hellenistic theology, not Judaism, which provides the only explanation to references concerning mysteries and secrets within Philo's writings, according to Reitzenstein.[22]

Reginald Fuller holds that it was Wilhelm Bousset who first theorized in his *Kyrios Christos* that the Hellenistic conception of the *theios anēr* was the basis for the derivation of the New Testament title "Son of God."[23] However, Bousset does not clearly link the concept of the divine man with Jesus or the title "Son of God." What he does is offer an extended discussion on the biblical title "Son of God," with the opinion that this title "does not at all fit in with the sensitivities of Old Testament piety . . . [for] It has a much too mystical ring which stands in contradiction with the rigid monotheism of the Old Testament."[24] Summarizing the biblical title he says,

---

[17]Tiede, 243.

[18]Richard Reitzenstein, *Hellenistische Wundererzählungen* (Neue Auflage, Darmstadt: Wissenschaftliche Buchgesellschaft, 1963), 50.

[19]Idem, *Die Hellenistischen Mysterienreligionen* (Neue Auflage, Darmstadt: Wissenschaftliche Buchgesellschaft, 1956), 12.

[20]Idem, *Hellenistische Wundererzahlungen*, 50, n. 1.

[21]Carl R. Holladay, *THEIOS ANER in Hellenistic-Judaism: A Critique of the Use of this Category in New Testament Christology* (Missoula, MT: Scholars Press, 1977), 26.

[22]Reitzenstein, *Die Hellenistischen Mysterienreligionen*, 37.

[23]Reginald H. Fuller, *The Foundations of New Testament Christology* (New York: Charles Scribner's Sons, 1965), 68-69.

[24]Wilhelm Bousset, *Kyrios Christos. Geschichte des Christusglaubens von den*

. . . where the title 'Son of God' comes to unquestioned prominence, that is, in the area of popular conceptions in the Gentile
Christian Church and in the Pauline-Johannine Christology,
there are bound up with it conceptions of a kind in part primi-
tively mythological, in part speculatively metaphysical, and these
simply have nothing more to do with a Christian messianology
which has its origin in Judaism.[25]

In a later discussion in the same work, Bousset comes closer to
identifying Jesus as a divine man. In a section devoted to the Apostle
Paul, Bousset introduces the subject of the divine man (θεῖος ἄνθρωπος). Using mystery religions as a comparison, Bousset discusses the
concept of ἐν χριστῷ and the new sociological idea implied in the eu-
charist. Bousset postulates that these betray something of the piety of
the Hellenistic mysteries.[26] In these religions, he points out, the
characteristic figure of the religious leader and wise man is as the
θεῖος ἄνθρωπος who alone stands firm in a tottering world, who is
leader and savior, pastor and pedagogue.[27]

The designation as θεῖος ἄνθρωπος is transferred from the leader
(mystagogue) to the follower (mystic) according to Bousset.[28] As the
follower who becomes new leader "in Christ," Paul the Apostle ap-
proaches the high sense of the θεῖος ἄνθρωπος, the religious superman.[29] By way of the Apostle Paul, Bousset implies that Jesus was
the original religious superman, savior, and wise man in the Christian religion. Jesus is thus a θεῖος ἄνθρωπος comparable to other such
figures in the Hellenistic world.

The first writer to specifically link the title "Son of God" with the
concept of the Hellenistic divine man was Gillis Wetter in his 1916
work *Der Sohn Gottes*. This work was so influential that Otto Betz
says it helped to create the belief that "Son of God" was to be equated
with the divine man.[30] The image of the divine man presented in
works such as Reitzenstein's provided the basis for Wetter to corre-

---

Anfanger des Christentums bis Irenaeus (Göttingen: Vandenhoeck & Ruprecht,
1913), 53.

[25]Ibid., 57.

[26]Ibid., 116.

[27]Ibid., 117.

[28]Ibid.

[29]Ibid., 118-19.

[30]Otto Betz, "The Concept of the So-Called 'Divine Man' in Mark's Christology," in *Studies in New Testament and Early Christian Literature*, ed. David
Edward Aune (Leiden: E. J. Brill, 1972), 231.

late with the portrayal of Jesus in John's Gospel.[31]
    In his work, Wetter made an extensive collection of parallels with the Hellenistic world. This, according to Nicol, was an attempt by Wetter to prove that John strove in his Gospel to convince Hellenists that Jesus was the real *theios anēr* by emphasizing his miracles.[32] Wetter saw the title "Son of God" as a known sociological type in the Hellenistic world, characterized as a wandering miracle-worker claiming to be sent from heaven by God.[33]
    The chapter in Wetter's book entitled "The Son of God as Miracle-Worker" deals in part with Jesus' knowledge of men's thoughts. Here Wetter refers to several examples of Jesus' ability to discern men's thoughts as recorded in John (e.g., 1:42, 47-50; 4:39; 16:30). With reference to the concept of "son of God," Wetter then says,

> Whoever clearly understands the ancient ideas will find that these thoughts will generally blend with that of the θεῖος ἄνθρωπος. The ability to discern the thoughts of men--which also is demonstrated later by the Christian spiritist (cf. e.g., 1 Cor. 14:24, 25), and in later Hellenistic times is seen in monks who, as nothing but itinerant beggar-prophets, exalted themselves--this is a characteristic which must be correlated along with the conception these men had of themselves. The ability to know in advance the day and hour of his death becomes one of the most powerful proofs regarding the individual as blending with God. This individual has gained entrance into the hidden decrees of the fathers and therefore has become completely divine, θεῖος. The trait of Jesus' omniscience, so often displayed in [John's] Gospel, is no doubt portrayed in the same manner (e.g. 6:6, 64, 70; 7:19; 8:21; 11:4, 9, 11, 15; 13:1f, 18; 16:19; 18:4, 32, etc.).[34]

Wetter held that the "son of God" figure was a popular Hellenistic concept that often correlated with that of the *theios anēr*. In the chapter entitled "The Son of God Comes from Heaven" he says,

> Up to now we have studied general traits in the son of God figure of the popular pious Hellenistic individual and found that the concept flows over into the θεῖος ἄνθρωπος, and in many re-

---

[31]Tiede, 243.

[32]Nicol, 49.

[33]Morton Smith, "Prolegomena to a Discussion of Aretalogies, Divine Men, the Gospels and Jesus," *Journal of Biblical Literature* 90 (1971):190.

[34]Gillis P. Wetter, *Der Sohn Gottes* (Göttingen: Vandenhoeck & Ruprecht, 1916), 71-72.. See Appendix for this quote in German.

spects is identical with it. We have seen how the concept began historically: out of phenomenally great feats, from mind-reading or similar acts, it can be concluded that θεῖοι have been called out with divine power, that their wisdom and higher awareness testifies to this, and that they are called 'gods.'[35]

Thus for Wetter the two titles, "son of God" and θεῖος ἄνθρωπος flow together with one another in Hellenism.[36]

There was a gap of ten years between Wetter's work and the next study dealing with the divine man. But in that time an eminent theologian indirectly contributed to the development of the divine man Christology.

Martin Dibelius' *Die Formgeschichte des Evangeliums*, which appeared in 1919, stressed the variety of traditions stemming from various sociological situations of the early Church. He also drew much attention to the miracle tales (*Novelle*) which he saw as similar to a variety of secular stories cultivated in popular Hellenistic traditions as propaganda for folk heroes.[37] He noted especially that the Jesus of these tales was not the herald of God's kingdom, but rather Jesus the thaumaturge.[38]

Dibelius compared these miracle tales of the Gospels with similar stories in the Hellenistic world. He held that this similarity indicated a popular form of literature which presented miracles as the authentication for an individual's divine status.[39]

The appearance in 1926 of Otto Weinreich's journal article "Antikes Gottmenschentum" marked an advancement in the attempts to find a general image of the Hellenistic divine man which might serve as a basis for early divine man Christology. Weinreich's method was to compile a list of features of various men in antiquity who were thought to have attained divine status (θεῖοι). He then compared this conglomerate image with Jesus.

Weinreich's article perused the concept of the divine man from Homeric times to the era of Celsus. In conclusion, of those who had been designated divine, he says the universal thought was that they rescued, helped, protected, taught, brought improvement, and served in general as "saviors."[40] He then turns to the person of Jesus and

---

[35]Ibid., 82-83. See Appendix for this quote in German.

[36]Ibid., 186-87.

[37]Tiede, 248.

[38]Martin Dibelius, *Die Formgeschichte des Evangeliums* (Tübingen: J. C. B. Mohr, 1933), 42-51.

[39]Ibid., 94-96.

[40]Otto Weinreich, "Antikes Gottmenschentum," *Neues Jahrbücher für Wis-*

asks,

> And yet, the question which burns in all our hearts is: How was the image of Christ understood in the ancient world? Was it perhaps the successor of some spontaneous analogous form? Was it truth or was it legend? Questions are more easily asked than answered.[41]

In the vein of Weinreich's method came Hans Windisch's *Paulus und Christus*. This work, along with Bieler's (which appeared one year later), represented the apex of the history-of-religions method of correlating the Gospel accounts of Jesus with the general image of the Hellenistic divine man.[42]

One third of Windisch's book is devoted not only to an exhaustive examination of the divine man, but also to that of the Old Testament "man of God."[43] His first and second chapters are entitled, "The θεῖοι ἄνδρες of Greco-Roman Antiquity" and "The Israelite Men of God and Their Hellenistic Interpretations," respectively. His contention is that the Old Testament heroes shared many of the traits of the Hellenistic *theioi*.[44] For Windisch, the Old Testament "men of God" were actually Israel's θεῖοι ἄνδρες.[45] He arrives at this by his analysis of how Hellenistic Jews (namely Philo and Josephus) appropriated the Old Testament presentation of "men of God." Philo and Josephus, by their depicting certain Old Testament figures as divine men, provide not only the link between Hellenism and Judaism, but also between Hellenistic Judaism and early Christianity.[46]

The basic assertion as reflected in the title, is that both Paul and Christ belonged to the Hellenistic type of divine man. Windisch says, ". . . new realizations overtook me, for a completely new aspect was opened to me during this time: 1) the similarity of both figures, the apostle-centered aspect of Jesus and the Christ-likeness of Paul and 2) the parallel of both figures with the 'man of God' of the Old Testament and of the *theios anthrōpos* of the Greco-Roman era."[47]

---

senschaft und Jugenbildung 2 (1926):650.

[41]Ibid. See Appendix for this quote in German.

[42]Tiede, 245.

[43]C. A. A. Scott, "Review of Windisch's *Paulus und Christus*," *Journal of Theological Studies* 36 (1935):85-86.

[44]Holladay, 27.

[45]Hans Windisch, *Paulus und Christus* (Leipzig: J. C. Hinrichs'sche Buchhandlung, 1934), 92.

[46]Ibid., 114.

[47]Ibid., v. See Appendix for this quote in German.

In his study, Windisch was aware of the apparent contrasts between the various divine men presented in ancient literature. Those contrasts were between the depictions of the divine philosophers and the divine miracle workers, both of which were sometimes labelled "divine men." In order for him to find a more idealized portrait of the divine man which might serve as a background to the Gospels' presentation of Jesus, he turned to Pythagoreanism.[48] Here he thought these different types were synthesized into an image which the gospel writers could employ. Of the Pythorean influence Windisch says,

> The state of his legend is not without significance for the understanding of Jesus and the history of his tradition and too few have pursued this theological facet. . . . And what is more, the tradition of Jesus stands substantially closer to the legend of Pythagoras, according to form and substance, than to the history or legend of a Jewish Messiah.[49]

Windisch also saw a link between the concept of the divine man and the title "son of God." To support this he points to the person of Alexander who Windisch says belongs to the *theioi*[50] and who was labelled "son of the gods Zeus and Amon."[51] Windisch then connects this to the person of Jesus and his being called "Son of God,"[52] implying that the two titles stand close together.

Although he provided an extensive study of the concept, Windisch said that more research was needed on the *theios anēr*.[53] That research came in the work of Ludwig Bieler.

Ludwig Bieler's Study

Perhaps the greatest contribution to the divine man Christology came from Ludwig Bieler. His study viewed massive amounts of material from the ancient world, spanning centuries of literature in the Greek

---

[48]Here Windisch demonstrates that he stands in the shadow of F. C. Baur. The latter sought to show the effect of Pythagoreanism on Judaism and Christianity, cf. *Apollonius von Tyana und Christus*, 216-27. Apollonius was indeed one of the key figures in neo-Pythagoreanism, cf. *Dictionary of Philosophy and Religion* (Atlantic Highlands, New Jersey: Humanities Press, 1980), s.v. "Pythagoreanism," by William L. Reese, 471.

[49]Windisch, 59-60. See Appendix for this quote in German.

[50]Ibid., 83.

[51]Ibid., 82.

[52]Ibid., 83.

[53]Ibid., v.

language. Very few of those who follow him fail to mention his study in their reference to the divine man concept. Helmut Koester says Bieler's work is still the standard.[54] His two-volume work, *ΘΕΙΟΣ ΑΝΗΡ*, appeared in 1935 and 1936. In these he analyzed material dealing with the lives of philosophers, sophists, legendary poets, monks, the Gospels and Acts, and literature from the first few centuries of the post-Christian era. The first volume amasses data arranged according to the various characteristics of the divine man, whereas the second volume cites examples of divine men from ancient literature.[55] From all of this, Bieler collected evidence about the divine man's life, character, appearance, supernatural knowledge, miraculous powers, teaching, followers, mission, relation to the surrounding world and relation to the gods.[56]

In this study, Bieler sought to find a composite portrait of the divine man. Toward the end of the first volume he says, "It should be an essential task of this work to show that the ancients, especially in late antiquity and early Christianity, had an identical understanding of the divine man."[57]

But the divine man concept was long in developing according to Bieler. It first was fixed in the age of Hellenism when it became somewhat commonplace in religions, and philosophical thought.[58] Yet even that fixed concept was not so rigid. Bieler says, "On the contrary, this [study] will abandon perceiving the common type, to some extent the Platonic idea of the ancient divine man, the one *θεῖος* who may never or nowhere be marked with the same essential traits merged into a final and consistent fulfillment, but rather one who, in each representative, possesses these traits more or less."[59]

Since Bieler's work deals primarily with the era of Christianity (cf. his subtitle, "Spätantike und Frühchristentum"), he allots only the first twenty pages to the divine man concept prior to this era. The *theioi* in Homer were of three classes: heroes, harbingers and

---

[54]Helmut Koester, "The Structure and Criteria of Early Christian Beliefs," in *Trajectories through Early Christianity* (Philadelphia: Fortress Press, 1971), 216, n. 20. Carl Holladay says, "To date Bieler still remains the source book of pagan passages regarded as evidence for *theios aner* . . ." 15, n. 25.

[55]Liefeld, 195.

[56]Smith, 192.

[57]Ludwig Bieler, *ΘΕΙΟΣ ΑΝΗΡ. Das Bild des "Göttlichen Menschen" in Spätantike und Frühchristentum.* (Reprint, Darmstadt: Wissenschaftliche Buchgesellschaft, 1976) 1:145. See Appendix for this quote in German.

[58]Ibid., 1:2-3.

[59]Ibid., 1:4. See Appendix for this quote in German.

kings.[60] The term is used overwhelmingly to refer to heroes, however. Thirty-one of the forty-six times Homer employs the term, he applies it to heroes.[61] Thus, as Bieler observes, "Whenever we encounter the word θεῖος [in Homer], we are in the sphere not [necessarily] of the religious, but certainly of the 'mysterious.'"[62]

In the centuries that follow Homer, the term continues to be used broadly. Even in Plato it has a "general meaning" (allgemeiner Bedeutung).[63] But in Aristotle the term becomes more concrete. In Aristotle and thereafter, Bieler sees the term *theios* as taking on a middle ground between the gods and men.[64] In fact, whereas the philosophical element grew weak, the religious element which grew out of philosophy, grew stronger.[65] In conclusion to his background study, Bieler says that only a "crude outline," of the divine man image was obtained, but nonetheless the concept which was evident pictured a man with humanly-measured outstanding qualities and abilities, who was favored by the gods and who was viewed as a middle species between God and men. He was a respected and successful individual [κατόρθωτης] towards whom many people gravitated.[66]

The concept narrows during the period following Aristotle and into the Christian era. Basically, Bieler sees two types of divine men here: the outstanding men and those who pass from the human sphere into the supernatural.[67] In the remainder of his first volume, Bieler devotes a chapter to each of the various characteristics of the *theios anēr*. The chapters peruse the events in the life of the divine man, the typical personality, his knowledge and ability, his teachings and works, his followers and schools, his acceptance or rejection, and his sonship to God. Bieler's purpose in this systematic arrangement is clear. Although he admits diversity among the various individuals, he seeks to assert that there was a generalized type of *theios anēr* which existed in the minds of people in the ancient world.[68]

Bieler includes the person of Jesus as part of this generalized picture. In chapter one, entitled "Typical Life Events," Bieler paral-

---

[60]Ibid., 1:10.

[61]Ibid.

[62]Ibid. See Appendix for this quote in German.

[63]Ibid., 1:14.

[64]Ibid., 1:16.

[65]Ibid., 1:17.

[66]Ibid., 1:20.

[67]Ibid., 1:23.

[68]Holladay, 30.

lels the portrait of Jesus with other divine men of antiquity. He compares the birth announcement of Jesus to other such accounts of divine men (1:22-26). He links the account of the young and unlearned Jesus teaching the elders together with secular accounts of *theioi* who taught others without themselves being schooled (1:35-36). Accounts of miracle-working, adversity, martyrdom, and even resurrection of divine men are compared with those events in Jesus' life (1:40-49).

Subsequent chapters continue the systematic examination of the typical divine man. In chapter two, "The Typical Personality," Bieler views the *theios anēr* with respect to his outward appearance, godliness, graceful speech, wisdom, humility and asceticism. Chapter three surveys the divine man's "knowledge and works," his ability to perform miraculous deeds, to know the hearts of men, to foresee the future and the time of his own death, to soar in the air and to walk on water. Chapter four, "Teachings and Works," examines the accounts of the divine man as the challenger and parable-teller, his works performed in public, his role as peace-maker, helper and counselor, his authority over nature (to work miracles of nature), and his role as founder of a cult. The divine man's acceptance and rejection, honor and scorn are viewed in chapter six.

In the first volume's seventh and final chapter, "God and God's Son," Bieler addresses the issue of the divine man's divinity. In a subsection called "The θεῖος ἀνήρ Descends from a God" Bieler says the divine man's relationship to divinity comes not only from his own claims, nor from those who believe in and follow him. Verification for the θεῖος ἀνήρ's divine nature comes from the miracles he performs, demonstrating him to be "the god in human form" (den Gott in Menschengestalt).[69] According to Bieler, the geneology of most miracle-working divine men can be traced back to find its origin in a god.[70] Furthermore, Bieler states that there are numerous instances where divine men have declared themselves or have been declared "god or son of a god."[71] Bieler offers no citation to substantiate this, however.

In the final pages of volume one, Bieler brings together the *theios anēr* as (a) god's son and the portrait of Jesus. He says,

> The Jesus of John's Gospel is distinguished very essentially from the former υἱοὶ θεοῦ, the θεῖοι ἄνθρωποι of Hellenism . . . because time and again he submits himself to the Father . . .

---

[69]Ibid., 1:134.
[70]Ibid.
[71]Ibid., 1:137. See Appendix for this quote in German

otherwise, however, John's picture of Christ emphasizes in particular the Hellenistic traits.[72]

According to Bieler, therefore, the portrait of Christ is a composite, one exhibiting traits which must be viewed collectively in order to be understood.[73] Jesus has no exact Hellenistic parallel, for he was set in a Jewish milieu which had an understanding of "son of God" long before Hellenism's impact.[74] But for Bieler the portrait of Jesus as depicted by the Gospel writers was influenced essentially by the Hellenistic concept of the divine man. Bieler repeatedly demonstrates this in his citing parallels between the portrait of Jesus and the divine man image.

In the conclusion to the first volume (pp. 140-50), Bieler attempts to sketch a general picture of the divine man. He says,

> First of all the θεῖος ἀνήρ is almost always said to be an unusual example of the congenial man, or as one might call him, a "superman," and indeed, in the direction of a religious hero. Hence there follows, above all, that he has a strong and fundamental linkage with the Divine. His life's work is service for God, to be a witness for the Deity. His knowledge comes directly from God, his teaching is divine revelation. His miracles [which] still may have some similitude of enchantment . . . are not magic . . . but theurgy. Often they plainly demonstrate direct discharge of divine power, which only goes through the divine man and is stored up in him as in a vessel. Thus the θεῖος ἀνήρ is a carrier of manna and as such enjoys religious veneration in life. As the ambassador of God he exercises miracle-working ability not as he himself wills, as do the magicians to the sport and delight of the people or to oblige overlords with his trick--a typical example of this is Jesus before Herod (Luke 23:8).[75]

The *theios anēr* is "often a man chosen by the deity, more often he is begotten by God, and at times he is himself (a) god."[76] Like the gods, he is equipped with miraculous gifts and abilities which he displays in order to produce reverence from the people.[77] The *theios anēr* suffers the same experience of rejection and scorn as a god who

---

[72]Ibid., 1:138-39. See Appendix for this quote in German.

[73]Ibid., 1:139.

[74]Ibid.

[75]Ibid., 1:141. See Appendix for this quote in German.

[76]Ibid., 1:142. See Appendix for this quote in German.

[77]Ibid.

appears on earth. But by persevering, the divine man triumphs after that suffering and receives glorification, as his work continues in his disciples.[78]

Bieler explains how he sees the development of the portrayal of Christ as a *theios anēr*. He asserts that portraits of certain individuals and their deeds escalated gradually into accounts of the miraculous as they were transmitted. These accounts were then applied to entirely different persons. This, says Beiler, is "a well-known fact" (eine bekannte Erscheinung).[79] It should be no surprise that this should happen in the case of Jesus, since he appeared in a time and a place when a subjugated people readily applied sketches of the miraculous to a powerful figure.[80]

The great diversity evidenced by the various divine men cannot be denied by Bieler. His explanation is that diversities of both the people and the time are responsible for the various portraits. This is the key to seeing Jesus as a *theios anēr*.

Jesus remains somewhat of a unique figure for Bieler. But the portrait of Jesus agrees with the religion of his time. And, although the basic image of the *theios anēr* is a fixed form, the content of the divine message which the *theios anēr* brings is dependent upon the setting in which he appears.[81] In other words, Jesus is historically no more unique than other divine men. He only appeared as such to a particular people and time.

For Bieler, there is a bifurcation between the Jesus of history and the Christ of faith. Historically, Jesus is a *theios anēr*. But Bieler does not want to admit a total lack of uniqueness for Christ, for that would mean the lack of uniqueness for Christendom. He claims that his study is a scientific approach, and cannot make judgments on religious matters.[82] Thus, concerning the person of Jesus, he says,

> For all those who knew Jesus, the great experience was especially the incredible escalation which his image experienced in their consciousness: from the rabbi Jesus who was crucified to the Kyrios Christos who arose. Whereas in Jewish as well as classical antiquity there was already a clear distinction between the divine men and the Godhead who walks on earth, Christ is both: θεῖος ἀνήρ in the eyes of his Hellenistic contemporaries, and

---

[78]Ibid., 1:143.
[79]Ibid., 1:148.
[80]Ibid., 1:145.
[81]Ibid., 1:149.
[82]Ibid., 1:150.

θεός ἐπιφανής in the faith of those who confess him.[83]

To whom is Bieler referring when he says Christ's "Hellenistic contemporaries?" He elaborates on this in his second volume.

Although Bieler admits that the Old Testament knew nothing of divine men,[84] yet he sees Hellenistic Judaism as bringing about a change. The Diaspora afforded more opportunity for contact with Hellenism and comparison with their ideas. It became easy to see the Old Testament men of God in a more Hellenistic light, i.e., as *theioi andres*.[85] The key examples Bieler gives in support of this assertion are the Jewish authors referred to by previous divine man advocates: Philo and Josephus.[86] Thus, for Beiler, the divine man concept was well-known to Hellenistic Jews during the lifetime of Jesus and is likely to be that which lies behind the New Testament portrait of Jesus.

Rudolf Bultmann's Transference Theory

Few theologians of the twentieth century have influenced so many areas in biblical studies and theology as Rudolf Bultmann. Of his importance Schubert Ogden says,

> Rudolf Bultmann is one of the most significant figures on the contemporary theological scene. By whatever criteria one judges such significance--whether quantitative or qualitative, whether with reference to specific areas of concern (i.e., "historical," "systematic," or "practical" theology) or to theological inquiry as a whole--his contribution is unchallengeably among the most important of our time. In the course of a long and productive scholarly career . . . he has come to be one of the most decisive influences on the direction of Protestant theology in the twentieth century.[87]

Bultmann's place in the development of the divine man Christology is that, in essence, he builds his own Christology on the concept of the Hellenistic divine man.[88] Because of his influence, this

---

83Ibid., 1:150. See Appendix for this quote in German.
84Ibid., 2:24-25.
85Ibid., 2:24.
86Bieler, 2:3-36
87Schubert M. Ogden, "Introduction," in *Existence and Faith: Shorter Writings of Rudolf Bultmann* (New York: Meridian Press, 1960), 9.
88Liefeld, 195.

fact has had extensive ramifications in the field of Christology.

As Ogden pointed out, Bultmann's expertise spanned more than one or two disciplines. His extensive knowledge made him adept at matching parallels in religions. Bultmann saw three major Hellenistic concepts lying behind the Christological title "Son of God." These three concepts were applied or transferred to Jesus in the Gospels. The first concept was the Near Eastern mystical son-deity which suffered the fate of human death but emerged as deliverer and *kyrios* of those honoring him. Second was the divine son of the Gnostic redeemer myth who sinks into the material world and releases the souls of the enlightened to the higher world. The *theios anēr* was the third concept transferred.[89] The first two have since been shown to be either anachronistic or essentially not looked upon as "sons of God" in Hellenism.[90] That of the *theios anēr* has remained.

Concerning the appearance and meaning of the New Testament title "Son of God," Bultmann says,

> The title "kyrios" was first conferred upon Christ in the Hellenistic Church. But Hellenistic-Jewish Christians brought along the title "Son of God" embedded in their missionary message, for the earliest church had already called Jesus so. But one must recognize that the title, which originally denoted the messianic king, now takes on a new meaning which was self-evident to Gentile hearers. Now it comes to mean *the divinity of Christ, his divine nature* [ital. his], by virtue of which he is differentiated from the human sphere; it makes the claim that Christ is of divine origin and is filled with divine power . . . While the term "Son of God" secondarily serves to differentiate Christ from the one true God and to indicate Christ's subordinate relation to God, it also serves--and this is the primary thing-- to assert his divinity.[91]

Several pages prior to this quote Bultmann asserts that neither Judaism nor the early Christian Church employed the title "Son of God" as the Hellenistic Christians did, i.e., that the "Son of God" is a supernatural being.[92] Therefore, the view that Christ as "Son of God" is a supernatural person is distinctively Hellenistic. Bultmann goes

---

89Rudolf Bultmann, *Theologie des Neuen Testaments* (Tübingen: J. C. B. Mohr (Paul Siebeck), 1958), 130-32.

90Leonhard Goppelt, *Theologie des Neuen Testaments* (Göttingen: Vandenhoeck & Ruprecht, 1976), 2:396-97.

91Bultmann, 130-31.

92Ibid., 53.

on to make this clear when he says,

> That the proclamation of "Christ, the Son of God," was so
> understood, is not to be wondered at; *the figure of a Son of God
> was familiar to Hellenistic ways of thinking* [ital his], familiar
> in several variations. One among them was an inheritance from
> the Greek tradition, which applied the mythological idea of being
> begotten by a god to men who seemed by their heroic deeds,
> mental accomplishments, or benefactions to humanity to tran-
> scend ordinary human proportions. The Hellenistic period
> knows a whole series of such "divine men" (θεῖοι ἄνδρες), who
> claim to be sons of (a) god or were regarded as such, and some of
> whom were also cultically worshiped. In their case, there is no
> emphasis, or almost none, on the paradoxicality of the divine
> appearing in human form; moreover, this was no problem at all
> to Greek thinking in general, for which every man's soul is a
> divine entity. Hence, here the interest lies not in the (para-
> doxical) fact of the divine son's humanity but in the content of
> his life (βίος) marked by miracles and other divinely conferred
> phenomena.[93]

Bultmann's penchant for matching parallels linked Hellenistic
literature with the Synoptics. Concerning this parallel he says, ". . .
the Hellenistic miracle stories offer such a wealth of parallels to the
Synoptic, particularly in style, as to create a prejudice in favor of
supposing that the Synoptic miracle stories grew up on Hellenistic
ground."[94] More specifically, Bultmann saw that, "The synoptic
gospels essentially represent the first type [of transference of Hellenistic 'son of God,' i.e. *theios anēr*] inasmuch as they picture Jesus as
the Son of God who reveals his divine power and authority through
his miracles."[95] As an example of this, Bultmann speaks of the
second evangelist's portrayal of Jesus,

> In Mark he is the θεῖος ἄνθρωπος, indeed more: he is the very Son
> of God walking on earth . . . But this distinction between Mark
> and Q means that in Q the picture of Jesus is made essentially
> from the material of the Palestinian tradition, while in Mark
> and most of all in his miracle stories, Hellenism has made a
> vital contribution. So naturally we can rightly assume in the

[93]Ibid., 132.
[94]Bultmann, *Die Geschichte der synoptischen Tradition* (Göttingen: Vandenhoeck & Ruprecht, 1957), 146.
[95]Idem, *Theologie des Neuen Testaments*, 132.

first place a Hellenistic origin for the miracle stories which Matthew and Luke have over and above those found in Q and Mark.[96]

Bultmann also saw the divine man concept operative in John's Gospel. Here the Old Testament Son of God and the θεῖος ἄνθρωπος come together in Jesus.[97] Jesus' knowledge of Peter's identity without previously meeting him, his ability to turn the water to wine, his supernatural knowledge of the woman at the well of Samaria, are all evidences that Jesus is the θεῖος ἄνθρωπος.[98] The Johannine Jesus is not a prophet in the Old Testament sense, as one whose supernatural knowledge and ability to perform miracles is given by God. Rather, Jesus is like the θεῖος ἄνθρωπος who exhibits such miraculous abilities because of his own personal divinity.[99]

By drawing more attention to the miracle stories which demonstrate Jesus' divinity, Bultmann narrowed the image of the divine man which had existed from Reitzenstein to Bieler.[100] His method followed in the form-critical approach of Dibelius and put more emphasis on the divine man as a miracle-worker.[101] Moreover, Bultmann emphasized the Hellenistic influence upon the Gospel accounts almost to the exclusion of Old Testament traditions.[102] For Bultmann, the Christianity reflected in the Gospels does not stem from the Old Testament, but is rather a Hellenistic Christianity representing a product of syncretism.[103]

Contemporary Adherents

As stated above, only the *theios anēr* facet of Bultmann's three-pronged transference theory remains. Goppelt says this is because the history of religions analyses out of which Bultmann developed this theory has been considerably revised by historical research.[104]

---

[96]Idem, *Die Geschichte der synoptischen Tradition*, 256.

[97]Idem, *Das Evangelium des Johannes* (Göttingen: Vandenhoeck & Ruprecht, 1959), 64, n. 3.

[98]Ibid., 70-71.

[99]Ibid., 71, n. 4.

[100]William L. Lane, "*Theios Aner* Christology and the Gospel of Mark," in *New Dimensions in New Testament Study*, ed. Richard N. Longenecker and Merrill Tenney (Grand Rapids: Zondervan Publishing House, 1974) 148.

[101]Tiede, 248.

[102]Ibid., 250.

[103]Bultmann, *Das Urchristentum im Rahmen der antiken Religionen* (Zürich: Artemis Verlag, 1949), 195-200.

[104]Goppelt, 2:396.

Rather than suffering the same fate, the *theios anēr* transference theory has gained momentum and been extended broadly.[105] Indeed, since the early 1960s a renewed interest has developed in the subject.[106] During this period, increasingly more writers have glibly referred to the concept as though it were proven fact. One of the first works to appear during this renewed interest was that of Hans Dieter Betz's *Lukian von Samosata und das Neue Testament*. Betz devoted much of this 1961 work to the concept of the divine man (göttlichen Mensch) but offered nothing essentially different from Bieler's study.[107]

In the same year Johannes Schreiber asserted in an analysis of Mark's Christology that the evangelist "reshaped" the divine man Christology from the traditional stories of exorcism and miracles. Schreiber's contention was that Mark sought to depict the cross, and not these other events, as the place where the Son of God decisively defeats the forces of Satan.[108] As shall be seen later, this contention was adhered to by others. It claimed that, although Mark did employ the tradition of the divine man and his miracles, he changed the focus of his Christology from a "theology of glory" to a "theology of the cross."[109]

Ferdinand Hahn's *Christologische Hoheitstitel* of 1963 is a good example of the continuation of Bultmann's theory. In the section "The Son of God Conception in Hellenistic Jewish Christianity," Hahn says one of the major concerns for his study is the "taking over of elements of the *theios anēr*-conception into the traditional Son of God concept."[110] Hahn's opinion is that the concept could not have "leaped" from pagan Hellenism into Christianity. It must have come via Hellenistic Judaism, for here the Old Testament "men of God" were put on par with the Hellenistic θεῖοι ἄνθρωποι[111] He supports this opinion with references to the use of the term *theios* by Josephus and Philo.[112] Therefore, Hahn contends, in pre-Christian times, Judaism of the Diaspora had already assimilated the Hellenistic idea of the *theios anēr* in connection with especially distinguished men endowed

---

[105]Ibid.

[106]Liefeld, 195.

[107]Ibid., 196.

[108]Johannes Schreiber, "Die Christologie des Markusevangeliums," *Zeitschrift für Theologie und Kirche* 58 (1961):154-83.

[109]Siegfried Schulz, *Die Stunde der Botschaft* (Hamburg: FurcheVerlag, 1967), 54-59.

[110]Ferdinand Hahn, *Christologische Hoheitstitel, Ihre Geschichte in frühen Christentum* (Göttingen: Vandenhoeck & Ruprecht, 1963), 292.

[111]Ibid., 293.

[112]Ibid., 294-95.

with God's power by his Spirit. Hellenistic Jewish Christianity then
picked this up and linked it with the person of Jesus.[113] The working
of miracles by Jesus was understood more in light of the Old
Testament charismatic person. Consequently, Hahn sees the
acceptance of the title Son of God as more closely linked with the Old
Testament.[114] Here Hahn carries Bultmann's theory further, for
Bultmann disputed the significance of the Old Testament tradition,[115] and never made it clear as to how he saw that transference to
have taken place from pagan Hellenism to Christianity.

The 1964 work of Dieter Georgi, *Die Gegner des Paulus im 2.
Korintherbrief*, presented a unique development in the divine man
Christology. Georgi held that the opposition to which Paul refers in 2
Corinthians stemmed from Hellenistic Jews who espoused a metaphysical viewpoint that men might share in the divine nature.
Georgi theorized that these men proved they were *theioi andres* by
working miracles.[116] Hellenistic-Jewish Christianity, having its
roots in Hellenistic Judaism, fused this metaphysical viewpoint with
the message of Christ. But their emphasis was upon Jesus as the
miracle-worker, the *theios anēr*, parallel to the figure of Moses
whom they held to be a *theios anēr*.[117] Because they were Christians,
Paul's opponents viewed themselves, by *Christus praesens*, as *theioi
andres* who can demonstrate their power by performing signs and
wonders. As an example from a Hellenistic parallel, Georgi refers to
Celsus's words in Origen's *Contra Celsus* 7.9, "I am God, or a son of
God, or a divine spirit. And already I have come, for already the
world is going to ruin, and you, O men, are to perish because of
iniquities."[118]

Georgi goes on to argue that the tradition about Jesus which
Mark inherited and which he recorded was that of the Hellenistic-
Jewish miracle-worker.[119] This hypothesis and the argument which
Georgi gave to support it has had much influence on the divine man
Christology. Kingsbury says,

> As for the situation-in-life in which the divine man tradition
> of Mark presumably emerged, the inclination has been simply to

---

[113]Ibid., 308.
[114]Ibid.
[115]Bultmann, *Die Geschichte der synoptischen Tradition*, 270.
[116]Dieter Georgi, *Die Gegner des Paulus im 2 Korintherbrief* (Neukirchen-
Vluyn: Neukirchener Verlag, 1964), 140-47.
[117]Ibid., 286.
[118]Ibid., 118.
[119]Ibid., 210, 213-16.

co-opt Georgi's description of the divine man heresy Paul faced in the A.D. 50s at Corinth and to postulate the same heresy as having afflicted the community out of which the Second Gospel eventually arose around A.D. 70. Justification for making this postulate is the hypothesis that itinerant Christian missionaries of Jewish-Hellenistic stripe spread the heresy of Corinth from place to place throughout the Roman Empire.[120]

Ernst Käsemann's 1965 study, *Exegetische Versuche und Besinnungen*, demonstrates agreement with Georgi. Käsemann says the portrait of the disciple in Matthew 10 shows one who bears the *theios anēr* by transference.[121] The evidence for this, Käsemann holds, is the comparative study of religions.[122]

Philipp Vielhauer offered an advancement for the development of the divine man Christology. He demonstrated the limitations of understanding the development of first century Christology when one focuses on Christological titles as Hahn and others had done. Vielhauer argued that the diversity of Christological viewpoints should be judged by analyzing the kinds of material in which that title appears, e.g. miracle accounts, sayings, etc. According to Vielhauer, the title "Son of God" in Mark's Gospel is used as both an eschatological royal title and, when it appears in miracle stories, as a synonym for *theios anēr*.[123]

In 1965 two journal articles by two different writers made similar assertions with reference to the divine man Christology of Mark. Following the "theology of the cross/theology of glory" dichotomy of Schreiber, Ulrich Luz and Leander Keck both held that Mark did indeed inherit the tradition of a Hellenistic divine man Christology associated with miracle stories. But rather than pass this tradition along or eliminate it, Mark sought to utilize these accounts to convey that the true glory of Jesus lay not in those miracles but in the cross.[124] Nevertheless, they still see the two concepts of "Son of God"

120Jack Dean Kingsbury, *The Christology of Mark's Gospel* (Philadelphia: Fortress Press, 1983.), 38.
121Ernst Käsemann, *Exegetische Versuche und Besinungen* (Göttingen: Vandenhoeck & Ruprecht, 1960), 2:101.
122Ibid.
123Philipp Vielhauer, "Erwagungen zum Christologie des Markusevangeliums," in *Aufsätze zum Neues Testaments* (München: Chr. Kaiser Verlag, 1965), 210-211.
124Leander E. Keck, "Mark 3,7-12 and Mark's Christology," *Journal of Biblical Literature* 84 (1965):341-58; Ulrich Luz, "Das Geheimnismotiv und die markinische Christologie," *Zeitschrift für die neutestamentliche Wissenschaft* 56 (1965):9-30.

and *theios anēr* as directly related, for Keck as says, "These miracles . . . are direct manifestations of the Son of God, and in a particular way--the *theios anēr*."[125]

The writings of Moses Hadas and Morton Smith have made contributions to the divine man Christology. In the 1965 work *Heroes and Gods*, Hadas sees aretalogy as a separate genre of literature in the ancient world. For him this is evident in the biographies of Pythagoras, Apollonius of Tyana, Philo's Moses and the Jesus of the Gospels.[126] In a separate work, Smith claims to see in Mark chapters 1-10 a collection of miracle stories which he calls, "an aretalogy of the divine man."[127] This classification is used by other key writers, as evidenced by H. D. Betz's contention that the term as used in the New Testament belongs to the technical vocabulary of aretalogy,[128] and by Helmut Koester's assertion that Mark's Gospel is but an adaptation of the literary genre called "aretalogy."[129]

The work of Theodore Weeden further developed Georgi's theory. But in Weeden's writings, the Gospel of Mark is the focus of study. According to Weeden, Mark wrote his Gospel in order to combat "false prophets" and "false Christs." These individuals proclaimed Jesus to be the great *theios anēr* who worked through them.[130] But even more, Weeden sees the disciples of Jesus as the original espousers of this position, for they progressed from imperceptibility, to misunderstanding, to abandonment of Jesus at the cross. Thus the *theios anēr* Christology, a theology of glory, had a lineage which began in the circle of disciples and made its way into a second generation community disheartened by continual suffering.

Weeden held that Mark refuted this heresy (and the challenge to his own leadership) by employing Jesus as his spokesman who espouses a theology of glory. Mark accomplishes this by first presenting a *theios anēr* portrait of Christ, then focusing on the true nature of Jesus' mission which is the cross. As Weeden says,

If the only portion of Mark's Gospel one possessed was 1:1--8:29,

---

125Keck, 350.

126Moses Hadas and Morton Smith, *Heroes and Gods* (New York: Harper & Row, 1965), 3, 101.

127Morton Smith, "A Prolegomena to a Discussion of Aretalogies, Divine Men, the Gospels and Jesus," 197.

128Hans Dieter Betz, "Eine Christus-Aretalogie bei Paulus (2 Kor 12, 7-10)," *Zeitschrift für Theologie und Kirche* 66 (1969):300, n. 69.

129Helmut Koester, "One Jesus and Four Primitive Gospels," in *Trajectories through Early Christianity* (Philadelphia: Fortress Press, 1971), 187-88.

130Theodore J. Weeden, "The Heresy That Necessitated Mark's Gospel," *Zeitschrift für neutestamentliche Wissenschaft* 59 (1968):153-55.

one would have to assume that Mark understood Jesus to be a *theios anēr* and that his messiahship was to be interpreted only within this perspective. There is absolutely no hint in the first half of the Gospel that authentic messiahship should contain any other Christological dimension.[131]

According to Weeden, then, everything in Mark through 8:29 portrays Christ as a *theios anēr*. This includes Peter's confession. Concerning this Weeden says, "Waving the red flag of *theios anēr* Christology, as he does, by introducing Jesus as the Son of God, saturating the first half of his Gospel with wonder-working activities of Jesus, and interspersing his own summaries of this *theios anēr* activity (1:32ff; 3:7ff; 6:53ff), Mark intends the reader to draw the only conclusion possible: Peter makes a confession to a *theios anēr* Christ."[132]

By the evaluation of Hans Dieter Betz, Jesus is to be viewed as the divine man par excellence.[133] For Betz, the concept is very obvious in the New Testament,

> As far as the New Testament is concerned, the technical term *theios anēr* is not applied to Jesus. However, since the concept can utilize a variety of honorific titles, the absence of the technical term itself is no conclusive argument against the presence of the concept. It was a Hellenistic-Jewish variation of the concept that influenced primitive Christianity, so that the presentation of Jesus naturally differs from that, for example, of Apollonius of Tyana.[134]

But, unlike Weeden, Betz does not see the suffering and death of Jesus as antithetical to the portrait of Jesus as a divine man. Rather, Betz sees a complexity of Christologies presented by the Gospel writers, each of these representing a different "version" of the divine man.[135] Here Betz seems to follow the broad portrait of the *theios anēr* painted by Bieler. In essence, Betz sees the *theios anēr* as equated with the title "Son of God." He says, "The title most prominent in Mark is "Son of God," a title for the Divine Man, now combined by Mark with the title for the eschatological messianic

---

131Idem, *Mark--Traditions in Conflict*, 56.
132Idem, "The Heresy That Necessitated Mark's Gospel," 148.
133Hans Dieter Betz, "Jesus as Divine Man," in *Jesus and the Historian*, 122-23.
134Ibid., 117.
135Ibid., 129-30.

king."[136]

In his *Grundriss der Theologie des Neuen Testaments*, Hans Conzelmann shows that he assumes the divine man Christology. In the section dealing with the pre-existence and incarnation of the Son he sees John describing Jesus' activity as the epiphany of the *theios anēr*.[137] Jesus proves that he is a *theios anēr*, according to Conzelmann, by demonstrating his supernatural knowledge and his great capacity to work wonders.[138] Thus, it is not necessarily the whole portrait of Jesus which corresponds with the *theios anēr*. Most important are those portions which show him demonstrating it, i.e., the "signs source."[139]

This "signs source" (*Sēmeiaquelle*) is the subject of some discussion for Jürgen Becker. He argues that in John's Gospel there is a rather primitive *theios anēr* presentation of Jesus which is part of the Johannine signs source. John corrected this, however, by presenting a more sophisticated "Revealer Christology" (*Epiphanienchristologie*).[140] The latter shows Jesus to be more than a mere miracle worker, for he is also the revealer of God to men.

Paul Achtemeier endeavored to demonstrate the presence of the divine man concept in the first century.[141] He attempted to show that the miracle stories of the New Testament "belong, in content and style, to the age in which they originated,"[142] by offering examples in both Jewish and non-Jewish literature. To support this he refers to accounts as recorded in the *Babylonian Talmud* which recorded miraculous events performed by the prayers of rabbis or by fictitious pious men.[143] Thus Jewish writings in the Hellenistic period place great emphasis on miracles and miracle-workers, and the category of "divine man" was a part of the Jewish tradition.

Like Weeden, Norman Perrin saw Mark in a Christological tension with the existing tradition. Perrin, who Kingsbury calls one of the most influential North American Marcan Scholars in recent

---

[136]Ibid., 122.

[137]Hans Conzelmann, *Grundriss der Theologie des Neuen Testaments* (München: Chr. Kaiser Verlag, 1968), 374-76.

[138]Ibid., 375-77.

[139]Norman Perrin, *The New Testament: An Introduction* (New York: Harcourt, Brace, Jovanovich, Inc., 1984), 225.

[140]Jürgen Becker, "Wunder und Christologie," *New Testament Studies* 16 (1970):130-48.

[141]Paul J. Achtemeier, "Gospel Miracle Tradition and the Divine Man," *Interpretation* 26:2 (1972):174-97.

[142]Ibid., 184.

[143]Ibid.

years,[144] saw that the title "Son of God" needed correction in the Gospel setting. Perrin contended that, as the tradition came to Mark, "Son of God" had divine man connotations.[145] Mark sought to correct this by employing the title "Son of man" and down-playing the common divine man picture. Perrin saw this tradition as one which presented Jesus as the miracle-working *theios anēr*, who manifests his power and authority through great feats.[146] This tradition persisted because,

> A crucified redeemer figure was "folly" in the Gentile world, because the characteristic redeemer figures in that world were either heroes of the mystery cults or "divine men." Hellenistic Jewish missionaries and Gentile Christianity met this problem by transforming Jesus into a "divine man" and his death into an apotheosis.[147]

Perrin's Christology is best summed up in his words,

> The historian of religion must necessarily concern himself with the general rather than with the particular, with what a text has in common with other texts than with what is unique to that text itself. It is of course essential both to take into account what a text has in common with other texts and also to learn what it is that is distinctive about the particular text. In the case of the gospel of Mark the historian of religion would readily recognize the presentation of Jesus as a miracle-working *theios anēr* in the cycle of stories . . . but then he would have to go on to recognize that in Mark these stories are being used in a quite particular way, namely to correct the Christology originally expressed in them.[148]

One of the most provocative works to appear in recent years in the theological milieu is the collection of writings entitled *The Myth of God Incarnate*. One critic of the work said it was no more than a resuscitation of nineteenth century liberal ideas of the person of

---

144Jack Dean Kingsbury, *The Christology of Mark's Gospel* (Philadelphia: Fortress Press, 1983), 31.

145Norman Perrin, "The Christology of Mark: A Study in Methodology," in *A Pilgrimmage in New Testament Christology*, revised edition, ed. Hans Dieter Betz (Missoula, MT: Scholars Press, 1974), 92-93, 112-113.

146Idem, "Towards an Interpretation of the Gospel of Mark," in *Christology and a Modern Pilgrimmage*, 35.

147Idem, *The New Testament: An Introduction*, 190.

148Idem, "Towards an Interpretation of the Gospel of Mark," 45.

Christ.[149] The essential question of each article and of the work as a whole is why the church of today should hold to the deity of Christ.

To help pose this question, one writer employs the concept of the *theios anēr*. In "Two Roots or a Tangled Mass?" Frances Young discusses the presence of the *theios anēr* concept in the portrayal of Jesus as an exceptional figure.

Young uses caution with the subject, pointing out that the approach of Bieler has "a number of weaknesses" and that, "It is therefore true, as many have pointed out, that *theios anēr* is by no means a fixed expression and there is no such thing as a specific and defined class of people commonly called 'divine men.'"[150] But this does not dissuade Young from seeing some connection between the concept and the Gospel picture of Jesus. She says,

> Yet for all the criticisms, the existence of striking analogies to Christology cannot be totally dismissed. We are confronted not just with the fact that anyone regarded as exceptional or outstanding in personality, power or status could be called *theios*, but with the fact that miraculous birth-stories, legends of extraordinary disappearance at death, acts of salvation and healing, deification and appearance from on high were not infrequently associated with such figures. . . . Whatever the weaknesses of the *theios anēr* theory, it cannot be denied that in the case of exceptional men, especially rulers and philosophers . . . the myths of the "immortals" were utilized to express a sense that they belonged, or had attained to a superior race and another realm; and since it is convenient to refer to this phenomenon by some agreed shorthand, the term *theios anēr* will continue to serve the purpose.[151]

The divine man Christology has been advocated most recently by James Robinson and Helmut Koester. In the introduction to a work authored by both men, Robinson sets forth the philosophy and intent of these two when he says,

> Both authors studied under Rudolf Bultmann. Both are involved in the current indigenization of the Bultmann tradition on

---

[149]Alasdair Heron, "Doing without the Incarnation?" *Scottish Journal of Theology* 31:1 (1978):71.

[150]Frances Young, "Two Roots or a Tangled Mass?" in *The Myth of God Incarnate*, ed. John Hick (Philadelphia: The Westminster Press, 1977), 100.

[151]Ibid., 101.

American soil.[152]

As disciples of Bultmann, these men assume, as did their mentor, the connection between the *theios anēr* concept in the Hellenistic world and that of the Christological title "Son of God." In a footnote to the statement "Jesus is the 'divine man' (*theios anēr*)," Koester says, "In the New Testament the titles *Christ* and *Son of God* [ital. his] are sometimes connected with the Christology of Jesus as the divine man."[153]

Koester holds that the sources behind the Gospels (at least for Mark and John) contain primarily miracle stories and that this "is widely recognized and needs no further debate."[154] According to Koester, these miracle stories are similar to secular accounts. He says,

> The conclusion of John's source is significant because it is typical [of aretalogies]. Similar conclusions are customary for [secular] books which recount the miraculous and powerful acts of great men or of gods.[155]

In reference to Mark's Gospel, Koester asserts that this work is an adaptation of the literary genre known as aretalogy.[156] Robinson sees this Gospel similarly, saying Mark's lengthy introduction "consists primarily in a collection of miracle stories . . . This cycle of miracle stories presents Jesus sufficiently in the role of a glorious *theios anēr*."[157]

Koester sees the divine man theology present in Luke-Acts,

> According to Luke, Jesus is the divine man. . . . The same theology of the divine man is even more blatantly present in the Lucan Acts of the Apostles.[158]

Of the Gospels and Acts Koester says,

152James M. Robinson, *Trajectories through Early Christianity* (Philadelphia: Fortress Press, 1971), 1.

153Helmut Koester, "One Jesus and Four Primitive Gospels," in *Trajectories through Early Christianity*, 188, n. 3.

154Ibid., 187.

155Ibid., 188.

156Ibid.

157James M. Robinson, "Kerygma and History in the New Testament," in *The Bible and Modern Scholarship*, ed. J. Philip Hyatt (Nashville, TN: Abington Press, 1965), 133.

158Koester, "One Jesus and Four Primitive Gospels," 191.

But these books do not simply seek to edify and minister to the popular desire to be entertained. However desirous of pious edification the mass of Christian people might have been, the basic theological and Christological conviction which made it possible to fulfill these desires was the same religious "divine man" motif that had already contributed to the success of Paul's opponents in 2 Corinthians.[159]

In 1980 Koester produced an introduction to the New Testament (*Einführung in das Neue Testament*). This work (dedicated to the memory of Rudolf Bultmann) marked the first comprehensive study on the whole New Testament which was permeated with the divine man presupposition.

As a background to the New Testament itself (chapters 1-6), Koester offers various examples of divine men prior to the first century. These examples include Lucian of Samosata and Alexander of Abonuteichus who "established a flourishing business with prophecies, healings, and advice in religious guise" and who were the "representation of divine power on the religious market in order to satisfy the desires and needs of human beings who no longer had a secure home in this world."[160] Koester gives other examples of those who had great wisdom and philosophy,[161] who mediated divine wisdom,[162] and who showed supernatural ability for leadership through insight, courage and dexterity.[163]

The divine man concept is applied to Jesus by Koester in each of the four Gospels. His first mention of the idea is in reference to the opponents of Paul in Corinth as seen in 2 Corinthians. Following Georgi's study, Koester says,

> The opponents of 2 Corinthians were Jewish-Christian missionaries . . . The methods employed by these new opponents originated in Hellenistic-Jewish propaganda and apologetics . . . This was accomplished through powerful deeds and miracles (12:11f), bragging about mystical experiences and the fulfillment of prayers (12:1-9), and spiritual exegesis (2 Cor. 3:4-18). These demonstrations were intended to make it possible to repeat the

---

[159]Ibid., 192.

[160]Idem, *Einführung in das Neue Testament* (Berlin: Walter de Gruyter, 1980), 179.

[161]Ibid., 276.

[162]Ibid., 288.

[163]Ibid., 304.

possession of divine power, as it had appeared in Moses or in Jesus, and thus to become a "divine man."[164]

Koester says that in Mark's Gospel, "Although Jesus still remained the divine man, this designation necessarily became a paradox in view of the suffering and death of the Son of Man who would appear on the clouds of heaven."[165]

Matthew is seen by Koester to have gone further in his estimation of Jesus. Koester says Matthew "attempts to remove the entire life, teaching, and actions of Jesus from the categories of the divine man . . . [as he] raises Jesus above the level of human or even super-human existence."[166] Koester sees John employing the divine man concept, however. Of this Gospel writer he says, "the tradition of miracle stories which appears in John as the Signs Source (*Semeia-quelle*) . . . is a collection of pieces from the Hellenistic propaganda in which Jesus is proclaimed as divine man."[167]

Finally, Koester sees Luke placing great importance upon Jesus as the divine man. He says, "Luke gives this motif new importance. Jesus is indeed the divine man who, empowered by the Spirit, accomplishes miraculous deeds and preaches the kingdom of God."[168]

Summary of the Divine Man Christology

The previous examination has demonstrated how the divine man Christology was born, grew and developed through this century. At the outset, the history of religions approach, with its effort to understand the New Testament in light of the historical context, saw the divine man idea having definite parallels to the portrait of Jesus Christ. F. C. Baur initiated the process with his comparison of Jesus and Apollonius of Tyana. The theory gained momentum with Reitzenstein's work. From that point onward certain scholars attempted to establish a correlation between Jesus and other men of antiquity who were said to have attained divine status. Of the development of the divine man Christology Lane says,

In seeking to demonstrate that a general conception of the divine man began to emerge in Hellenism, which furnishes a para-

---

164Ibid., 561.
165Ibid., 610-11.
166Ibid.
167Ibid., 622.
168Ibid., 753.

digm for the portrayal of Jesus in the gospels, they appealed primarily to accounts of charismatic figures . . . under the impulse of discovering a general Hellenistic image of the divine man which could expose the Hellenistic framework of early Christology, they compiled a list of features which were variously ascribed to men who were thought to have attained divine status. This conglomerate was then set in juxtaposition to the gospel tradition about Jesus.[169]

When Lane says, "the general Hellenistic image of the divine man" he refers to what adherents saw as common to the divine man picture as a whole. Although Bieler admitted diversity among the various individuals who were so-called, yet he saw a generalized picture of the *theios anēr*. This is reflected most recently in Koester's words. Concerning the "symbol" of the divine man he says,

> The context of this symbol is the Hellenistic belief that divine power can be present in certain charismatic human beings. This belief has found literary expression in a number of biographies of the Roman period, most of all the *Life of Apollonius of Tyana* by Philostratus, *The Life of Alexander* by Pseudo-Kalliothenes, several lines of Augustus (Suetonius and Nikolas of Damascus) as well as Lucian's satirical lives of Peregrinus Proteus and the fake prophet Alexander.
>
> However, at the root of these literary productions are actual beliefs in the presence of divine power, as well as actual claims made by prophets, miracle workers, and wandering philosophers to possess such supernatural abilities. It is documented in skilled and persuasive oratory, miraculous healings and exorcisms, ecstatic visionary experience, and the like--and legend was only too quick to add wonderful stories about miraculous events at the birth and the death of a divine man.[170]

Koester goes on to relate how Jewish apologists such as Philo and propagandists like Paul's opponents made use of this concept.[171]

But how did the divine man concepts become linked with the portrayal of Jesus in the New Testament? Edwards gives a succinct explanation,

---

[169]Lane, 147.

[170]Koester, "The Structure and Criteria of Early Christian Beliefs," in *Trajectories through Early Christianity*, 216-17.

[171]Ibid., 217.

Stated in a simple way, the position holds that the earliest
Messianic titles, i.e., "Messiah," and "Son of Man," came from
the Jewish-speaking milieu and reflect a Jewish-Old Testament
understanding of Jesus. When the kerygma began to flow out of
Palestine and into the Hellenistic world . . . such titles became
foreign and meaningless to Hellenistic man, and new ones were
needed to communicate the meaning of Jesus. Hellenistic titles
and concepts were thus adopted, among them "Lord" and "Son of
God," in an attempt to convey an adequate, understandable
Christology.[172]

What Edwards described is said to have entered the Gospel tradition
via Mark. Kingsbury explains,

Since Mark appears to have written his Gospel in a Hellenistic
setting, it can be assumed that he was familiar with this concept
of divine man. Indeed, to proclaim Jesus effectively or to instruct
or edify Christians, Mark could be expected to have draped Jesus
in the cloak of the divine man. Hence, from all indication it
would seem that exactly the Hellenistic concept of divine man
provides the best avenue of approach for gaining insight into
Mark's presentation of Jesus.[173]

Mark's Gospel holds such importance, of course, because it is
commonly viewed as the earliest Synoptic. So pervasive is the divine
man Christology in Markan scholarship that Lane says,

Although the question continues to be debated whether the
primary locus of a *theios anēr* depiction of Jesus is the pre-
Markan tradition or the gospel of Mark itself, there is a general
tendency in German and American scholarship to assume that
a *theios anēr* Christology is inherent within the miracle tradition and records of controversy in Mark 1-8 and within the
strands of the Markan passion narrative. The particular reading of the evidence and the *theios anēr* configuration recognized
within the text varies, but the assumption is scarcely questioned
that behind the gospel of Mark lies a Hellenistic view of Jesus
which is indebted to the image of the *theios anēr* as a miracle-

---

172James Robert Edwards, "The Son of God: Its Antecedents in Judaism and
Hellenism and Its Use in the Earliest Gospel," (Ph.D. dissertation, Fuller Theological Seminary, 1978), 126.

173Jack Dean Kingsbury, "The 'Divine Man' as Key to Mark's Christology,"
Interpretation 35:3 (1981):243-44.

worker.[174]

The accepted theory as to how the Hellenistic concept made its way into the Early Church is that it came via Hellenistic-Jewish writers such as Philo and Josephus.[175] These men applied the divine man concept to such Old Testament figures as Moses, thus assimilating Hellenistic concepts into the Old Testament tradition.

The work of those who came before Bultmann provided the foundation for his transference theory. Many who followed may have been drawn to the divine man approach because of Bultmann's work. Not one of the divine man advocates examined for this study questioned the validity of the transference theory. Thus, although the transference theory itself has not been propounded, the *theios anēr* Christology, which is a vital part of it, has gained in popularity.

The latest and most prolific advocates of this Christology are disciples of Bultmann. Whereas the other two prongs of the transference theory have been refuted and have passed from the scene, the divine man transference lives on.

The ability to perform miraculous deeds, to tell the future, to manifest wisdom, etc. is attributed to Jesus as to the other figures in the ancient world. The word *theios* has been used in Greek literature from the 8th century B.C. to the 3rd century A.D. Within this millennial span lived the historical figure, Jesus Christ. If this term stands behind the Christological title "Son of God," perhaps Jesus is to be seen as just another charismatic figure in history.

Further investigation is therefore needed. The biblical title "Son of God" must be examined. This is the objective of the next chapter.

---

[174]Lane, "*Theios Aner* Christology and the Gospel of Mark," 148-49.
[175]Holladay, *THEIOS ANER in Hellenistic-Judaism*, 15-17.

2

The "Son of God" Concept
in the Old Testament

This chapter and the next will seek to establish the meaning of the biblical title "Son of God" as applied to Jesus. To do so, the Old Testament use of the concept must first be studied, since it stands as a possible background to the New Testament title.

This is not an exhaustive examination. A thoroughly comprehensive study of the title "Son of God" is beyond the scope of one book. However, enough material will be reviewed so that a comparison might be made with the divine man Christology.

The examination of the biblical concept "Son of God" in each of the Testaments will proceed in three stages. These stages might be visualized as three concentric circles. The outer circle deals with the general idea of sonship as used in the Old Testament to express some level of a relationship or association. The middle circle holds the more specific subset expressing "sonship to God" or "filial relationship and obedience to God." The inner-most circle corresponds to the unique sonship of Israel's Messiah.

It is only reasonable that an examination of the Old Testament concept of the "Son of God" should precede any consideration of its use in the New, since the New Testament as a whole makes such frequent references of the Old. Thus the effort to gain an understanding of the "Son of God" in the minds of the first century hearers--and Palestinian Jews in particular--will begin with a study of the concept in the Old Testament. This examination begins with the outer-most of the concentric circles: the general idea of sonship.

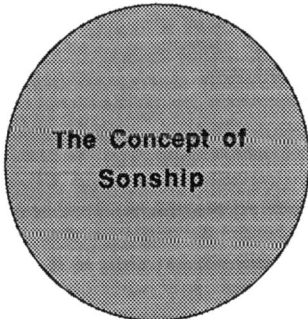

The Concept of Sonship

Sonship: the various concepts

In order to understand properly the concept of sonship to God in the
Old Testament, the use of the term "son" (בֵּן) must first be understood. The word is employed with much variety in the Old Testament.
In the sense of physical offspring, the term is used to speak not only
of immediate descendants, but also of grandsons, remote descendants, and sons-in-law.

Several concepts were inherent in the literal use of sonship in the
Old Testament. As in the rest of the Semitic world, childlessness was
bad (Gen. 30:1; 1 Sam. 1:11) and was even considered to be a form of
divine punishment (Gen. 20:18; Lev. 20:20). In particular, sons are
desired because they carry on the name of the father and the family.[1]
Thus,

> The life of a father has meaning only insofar as it is continued in
> his son (Gen. 15:2). . . . A son keeps the name of his father from
> being forgotten.[2]

In this vein, the rabbis regarded the childless man as dead.[3]

Because the father's life is seen as continuing in his son, the
latter's very existence has two functions. The son carries on the
father's name, but he also carries on or reflects the father's image.
This introduces an important aspect of sonship in the Old Testament:
obedience. Only as the son obeys his father's teaching and commands
can he properly carry on that image. The Old Testament, and Proverbs in particular, stresses the need for the son to heed the teaching
of his father (e.g., Prov. 1:8; 4:1; 6:20; etc.)

The Old Testament does not limit the use of sonship to that of
physical offspring, however. As Martin Hengel summarizes, "In
contrast to υἱός [in the New Testament], bēn in the Old Testament not
only (or even primarily) designates physical descent and relationship, but is a wide-spread expression of subordination, which could
describe younger companions, pupils and members of a group, membership of a people or a profession, or a characteristic."[4] Hengel goes
too far when he says the term denotes "subordination." It sometimes

---

[1]Bruno Meissner, *Babylonien und Assyrien*, (Heidelberg: Carl Winters
Universitätsbuchhandlung, 1920) 1:394.

[2]*Theological Dictionary of the Old Testament*, trans. John T. Willis, ed.
Geoffrey W. Bromiley, s.v. "בֵּן," by H. Haag, 2 (1977):154.

[3]*The Jewish Encyclopedia*, ed. Alfred M. Friedenberg, s.v. "Child, the," by A.
M. Friedenberg, 4:27.

[4]Martin Hengel, *The Son of God*, trans. John Bowden (Philadelphia: Fortress
Press, 1976) 21.

does, but in all the metaphorical uses, this meaning is rare.[5] His statement may stem from the fact that in the literal and some of the figurative uses, the "son" is he who receives instruction and vocational, moral and religious training.[6] Yet Hengel is accurate in his observation with regards to "sonship" expressing relationship or similarity of characteristics.

As the following pages will show, there are three levels of relationship represented by the use of the construct "son of" with the word in the genitive case. The first level is that which expresses a general "association with," while the second connotes "likeness to." The third--similar to the second but going somewhat further--speaks of the "son" as one who shares the same nature with that which is represented by the word in the genitive case.

The first level, a general "association with" expresses "membership of a people, country or place."[7] Often sonship is used to identify inhabitants of a particular country. Examples of this include "sons of Asshur" who are the Assyrians (Ezek. 23:7); "sons of Babel" are the Babylonians (Ezek. 23:15); "sons of Edom" are Edomites (Ps. 137:7); "sons of Judah" are the Jews (Joel 3:6); and of course "sons of Israel" are the Israelites (Exod. 3:9 ff.; Lev. 1:2 ff., etc.).

This term of association is applied to other concepts besides geographical location or nationality. Often the father-son terminology is employed where a non-physical yet close bond exists between two persons. The elder (or "superior") is seen as "father" while the younger (or subordinate) is seen as the "son."[8] Examples of this usage include Eli's reference to Samuel (1 Sam. 3:6); Saul's address to David (1 Sam. 24:16); Joshua's address to Achan (Josh. 7:19); and Ahaz's reference to himself as Tiglath-pileser's "servant and son" (2 Kings 16:7).

The second level of relationship expressed by metaphorical sonship is that of "likeness to" or "similarity with." The relationship at this level connotes membership in a special "group or fellowship."[9]

---

[5]*Theological Dictionary of the New Testament*, trans. Geoffrey Bromiley, ed. Gerhard Kittel and Gerhard Friedrich, s.v. "υἱός," by Georg Fohrer, 8 (1972):345.

[6]Ibid., 343.

[7]Ibid., 346.

[8]The father-son terminology (as shall be seen later in this study) was frequently employed in the ancient Near East to express this manner of association and is the language used in Oriental suzerainty-vassal treaties. See J. M. Munn-Rankin, "Diplomacy in Western Asia in the Early Second Millennium B.C.," *IRAQ* 18 (1956):76, 80 and William L. Moran, "The Ancient Near Eastern Background of the Love of God in Deuteronomy, "*Catholic Biblical Quarterly* 25 (1962):77-87.

[9]Fohrer, 345.

Examples here include "sons of the poor" = poor individuals (Ps. 72:4); "sons of the priests" = priests (Ezra 2:61); "a son of a prophet" = a prophet (1 Kings 20:25); "son of a stranger" = a foreigner (Exod. 12:43); "a son of the wise" = a wise man (Isa. 19:11). The writer of Proverbs exhorts the listener ("my son") to obey his wise counsel that he too might be wise (2:1; 3:1, 21; 4:10, 20; 5:1; 6:1; 7:1). The "son" in Proverbs is not necessarily to be seen as the speaker's literal offspring. As Delitzsch says, the teacher can be seen as a "fatherly friend."[10]

The essence of the relationship connoted in the third and final level is that of the "sharing of a nature or quality."[11] Here the construct "son" is practically the same in essence as the entity expressed in the genitive. Examples of this usage include "sons of rebellion" = rebels (Num. 17:10); "sons of worthlessness" = worthless men (Deut. 13:14); "sons of wickedness" = wicked men (Hos. 10:9); "son of a murderer" = a murderer (2 Kings 6:32); "sons of fire" = sparks (Job 5:7); and many examples of "son of man" = a man (Job 25:6; Ps. 8:4; Isa. 51:12; etc.).

This brief survey has given but a few examples of each of the three levels of the metaphorical use of sonship in the Old Testament. To be sure, the usage could be broken down into more than three areas.[12] But these three are sufficient to encompass the Old Testament's metaphorical use of sonship.

To summarize this examination of the Old Testament use of sonship, the literal concept connotes the carrying on of the father's name with the responsibility to bear the father's image and reflect his character. This is accomplished when the son demonstrates loyalty to his father and obeys his commands.

The metaphorical use expresses an association between entities. That association may be a relatively loose one (e.g., an arrow is a "son of the bow," Job 41:28), or it may be much closer in relation so that a similarity exists between the two (e.g., "son of a stranger" is a foreigner). But sonship might also convey the idea that the two entities in the association are identical in nature. Hence the term בֵּן sometimes is employed to describe the essence of the person or thing.

The next two sections examine how the Old Testament employs both the literal and metaphorical concepts of sonship to connote sonship to God. The section which follows will deal with the more general concept of sonship to God in the Old Testament.

---

[10]Franz Delitzsch, *Proverbs, Ecclesiates, Song of Solomon,* trans. M. G. Easton, reprint ed. (Grand Rapids: William B. Eerdmans, 1973), 59.

[11]Fohrer, 346.

[12]Fohrer (345-47) mentions five, while ten metaphorical uses for the term בֵּן are listed by Haag, 149-53.

Sonship: God as Father

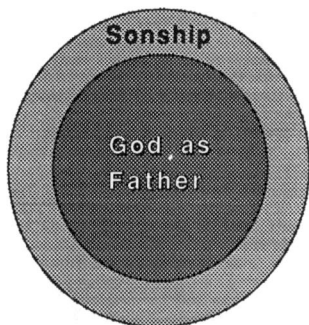

Although the Old Testament never uses the formula אֱלֹהִים בֶּן ("son of God"), the concept of sonship to God is seen in three ways. The first usage is with reference to heavenly or angelic beings ("sons of God"). The second concerns the Israelite people (God calls Israel "my son"and Israel refers to him as "Father"). The third usage (which will be examined in a separate section) refers to the king or the Messiah of Israel (God says "he will be a son to me"). The usage which refers to angelic beings as sons of God will be examined first.

The terms בֶּן and בַּר are sometimes used by the Old Testament to refer to beings which belong to and function with God in the superhuman sphere. The phraseology varies from passage to passage. Examples of this variation include: בְּנֵי הָאֱלֹהִים in Gen. 6:2,4; Job 1:6; 2:1; 38:7; בְּנֵי אֵלִים in Ps. 29:1 89:7; and the Aramaic בַּר אֱלָהִין Dan. 3:25. Although opinions vary as to who the "sons of God" are in Gen. 6:2-4, Gerald Cooke says, "It is difficult to avoid the impression that these . . . are to be understood as essentially divine beings rather than ancient heroes."[13]

But why are the angels called "sons of God?" Brendon Byrne holds that sonship here "should be taken in the common Semitic usage of 'son' to denote membership of a class or group" so that these beings belong to "the divine sphere."[14] Cooke concurs with this, concluding in his study on angels as "sons of God" that they are "lesser divine beings."[15] Byrne's conclusion is that angels are divine because they "remain sharers of God's home, his holiness, his nature."[16]

The last assertion may seem like an overstatement, unless it is seen as a comparison. With respect to man, angels may indeed be viewed on the "divine side" of creation. The Old Testament says nothing of any physical relationship between God and the angels as

---

[13]Gerald Cooke, "The Sons of (the) God(s)," *Zeitschrift für die alttestamentliche Wissenschaft* 76 (1964):23-24.

[14]Brendon Byrne, *"Sons of God--Seed of Abraham"* (Rome: Biblical Institute Press, 1979), 10.

[15]Cooke, 36.

[16]Byrne, 15.

"sons" as is found in other cultures of the ancient Orient.[17] Yet they do remain separate from the human sphere in their activity and holiness. Cooke says that since the sonship of angels is not to be taken in any filial sense,[18] it must be essentially functional.[19]

This functional sonship is a part, but not all, of the meaning of sonship of God for angels. It seems there are three reasons for their being so-called. The first is that they are direct creations of God. There is no progenitor in the case of the angels except for the Creator, himself. Each is the direct result of the creative activity of God.[20] Secondly, and as a consequence of the first, they are to some extent a reflection of God. Unlike man, who fell into sin, the holy angels who remained true to God did not "leave their first estate" but remained in the state in which God had created them. Thus they may be described as being on the "divine side" of creation. Finally, they are "sons of God" because of their function. They serve God and operate in the super-human heavenly sphere because of the power delegated to them by God.[21] This is a class or group occupied by no man. Angels functioned with God at creation and were often employed as messengers and instruments of his will throughout the Old Testament. Therefore, angels can be seen as "sons of God" because they bear the image of God and because they function in the divine sphere. Because of this they enjoy an association with God which may be viewed as "membership in a special group or fellowship."

Obviously sonship for Israel has a somewhat different application. Nowhere in the Old Testament is God seen as the progenitor of this nation.[22] Why was this concept used with reference to Israel?

Although Byrne argues to the contrary,[23] the sonship of Israel stands as an important theme in the Old Testament. In the foundational books of the Pentateuch, the concept occurs several times. When Israel was in bondage to Egypt, Yahweh referred to his people as "my son, my firstborn" (Exod. 4:22-23). In Deuteronomy, Israel's sonship is a very important motif. Here their sonship or God's Fatherhood is referred to six times (1:31; 8:5; 14:1; 32:5, 6, 18).

17Fohrer, 348.

18Cooke, 24.

19Ibid., 25.

20In Lk. 3:38 the first man Adam is called the "son of God" for the same reason. He had no earthly father as did the others listed in the geneology, so he was the immediate creation of and image of God.

21*Cyclopedia of Biblical, Theological and Ecclesiastical Literature*, ed. John M'Clintock and James Strong, s.v. "Son," by B. Pick, 9:875.

22Joachim Jeremias, *The Prayers of Jesus*, trans. John Bowden, Christoph Burchard, and John Reumann (Naperville, IL: Alec R. Allenson, Inc., 1967), 12.

23Byrne, 16.

Deuteronomy is of great importance due to the hortatory nature of Moses' address designed to move the people to obedience.[24] It is a book whose influence on religious life is, according to J. A. Thompson, unsurpassed by any other Old Testament book.[25] The later prophets Isaiah (1:2; 45:11; 63:16; 64:8), Jeremiah (3:19; 31:9), Hosea (11:1; 13:3) and Malachi (1:6; 2:10) all acknowledge the sonship of Israel. Thus the sonship motif must have been a very significant one for the covenant people of Israel.

The existence of the covenant points up the most obvious aspect of the fatherhood of God. There is nothing unique about an ancient Near Eastern culture viewing its god as "father," "shepherd," or "king," as Israel did with Yahweh.[26] This is only natural, says Eichrodt, since a king needs subjects and a father needs children. Such ideas make the deity dependent upon the worshipers. But the uniqueness for Israel, Eichrodt notes, comes in the concept of the covenant which denies the pagan use of those ideas.[27] The covenant means that Yahweh is Israel's only God, who stands as an authoritative, loving, and providing father.[28] Israel is thus the son because they are the object of God's special favor,[29] and must respond in obedience.[30] Moreover, as Joachim Jeremias points out, unlike other instances of a god being called "father" in the ancient world, Yahweh demonstrated that Israel was his son by the historical act of deliverance from Egypt.[31] Thus Israel's sonship is unique in the ancient Near East, being grounded in history, not in mythology.

The father-son language of Deuteronomy mirrors the terminology in ancient Oriental suzerainty-vassal treaties,[32] where sonship

---

[24]Peter C. Craigie, *The Book of Deuteronomy* (Grand Rapids: William B. Eerdmans, 1976), 17.

[25]J. A. Thompson, *Deuteronomy: An Introduction and Commentary* (Downers Grove, IL: InterVarsity Press, 1974), 11.

[26]Walther Eichrodt, *Theology of the Old Testament*, trans. J. A. Baker (Philadelphia: Westminster Press, 1961), 1:67. Cf. Num. 21:29 where the Moabites refer to their god Chemosh as "father."

[27]Ibid., 1:67.

[28]Ibid., 1:235-36.

[29]Gerald Cooke, "The Israelite King as the Son of God," *Zeitschrift für die alttestamentliche Wissenschaft* 73 (1961):217.

[30]H. Haag, "Sohn Gottes im Alten Testament," *Theologische Quartalschrift* 154 (1974):226-27.

[31]Jeremias, 13.

[32]Dennis J. McCarthy, "Notes on the Love of God in Deuteronomy and the Father-Son Relationship between Yahweh and Israel," *Catholic Biblical Quarterly* 27 (1965):144-47.McCarthy's work is based on the findings of William L. Moran, "The Ancient Near Eastern Background of the Love of God in Deuteronomy," *Catholic Biblical Quarterly* 25 (1963):77-87.

expressed the subordination and expected obedience of a vassal to his overlord "father."[33] Deuteronomy is a key book in this discussion because of the number of references to the fatherhood of Yahweh and because of Deuteronomy's similarity to ancient Near East treaty language.[34] Dennis McCarthy sees the father-son formula in Deuteronomy functioning similarly to that of ancient suzerainty-vassal treaties, thus making Israel's sonship essentially a matter of obedience.[35]

Many writers concur with McCarthy's view.[36] Indeed, the use of the father-son motif is frequently employed in Old Testament passages where the prophet assails the disobedience of Israel (Deut. 32:5, 6, 18; Isa. 1:2; Hos. 11:1; Mal. 1:6; 2:10). It certainly does not run counter to the idea of sonship to see it including obedience. But is Israel's sonship to be summed up in the concept of obedience?

To begin answering this, consideration is first given to Moshe Weinfeld's contention with McCarthy's view. Of the three passages in Deuteronomy (1:31; 8:5 and 14:1) which describe the Yahweh-Israel relationship as one of father and son, Weinfeld says,

> Only the last may be regarded as having an actual treaty setting.
> . . . McCarthy supposed that all three passages have a treaty background. But even in Deut. 14:1 we cannot be sure that the image is taken from the treaty sphere.[37]

Thus, although the Deuteronomy passages may seem to mirror ancient Oriental treaty language, something more may be implied in the use of the father-son formula as the Old Testament uses it.

The father-son imagery should not, in fact, be seen as a part of the covenant made at Moab prior to entering Canaan (Deut. 29). Because, if the essence of Israel's sonship entailed only obedience, then they would have forfeited that sonship early in their history. But even the obstinate disobedience which Israel demonstrated does not cause God to disown them. Throughout their history, the prophets

---

[33]Munn-Rankin, 76-80.

[34]*Theological Dictionary of the Old Testament*, s.v. "בְּרִית," by Moshe Weinfeld, 2:266-67.

[35]McCarthy, 145-46.

[36]*Theological Handworter zum Alten Testament*, ed. E. Jenni and Claus Westermann, s.v. "בֵּן," by Joachim Kühlewein, 1 (1971):323; *Theological Dictionary of the Old Testament*, s.v. "אָב,"by H. Ringgren, 1 (1974):18; H. Haag, "Sohn Gottes im Alten Testament," *Theologische Quartalschrift* 154 (1974):223-31; Walther Eichrodt, *Theology of the Old Testament* 1:243.

[37]Moshe Weinfeld, *Deuteronomy and the Deuteronomic School* (Oxford: Clarendon Press, 1972), 368-69, n. 6.

refer to them as God's "son," even to the final book of the Old Testament canon (Mal. 1:6; 2:10; 3:17).

That Israel's sonship is not simply to be equated with obedience can be seen in two other ways. First, as O'Connell notes, by God's calling and demonstration of care, Israel is already a "consequenced people," and the concept of sonship cannot be achieved by purely human effort.[38] Obedience is but a response.[39] Yahweh had called Israel his "son" before Sinai and the covenant, and before the writing of Deuteronomy and its use of treaty language (Exod. 4:22).[40] Secondly, unlike the despotic overlords of the ancient world, God's commands for obedience stem from a benevolent heart. He desires obedience in like manner.[41] God's moral demands, Driver notes, stem from Israel's being called "son" and not vice-versa.[42] That is, God's calling and God's love for Israel are the basis for Israel's sonship, and this precedes the call to obedience.

Therefore, the obedience to which Israel is called does not determine sonship, but is rather a consequence of it. Thus God's demands for obedience are seen to have purpose.

This purpose stems from the call of God. God "begat" Israel (Deut. 32:18) as his "firstborn" (Exod. 4:22) and called Israel out of Egypt as a father beckons his son (Hos. 11:1).[43] This is the basis for the covenant and for God's requirement that Israel respond in obedient love by recognizing him as their only God (Deut. 6:5; Exod. 20:3). The foundation for this obedience, however, is Israel's unique association with Yahweh referred to in terms of a filial relationship. This did not mean, of course, that Yahweh was the literal progenitor.[44] Yet the filial terminology is so often employed that Israel's sonship, though not literal, parallels a physical relationship. As a son resembles his father, Israel is to resemble Yahweh in a moral sense. God

---

[38]Matthew J. O'Connell, "The Concept of the Commandment in the Old Testament," *Theological Studies* 21 (1960):372.

[39]Hans Walter Wolff, *Hosea*, trans. Gary Stansell (Philadelphia: Fortress Press, 1974), 197-98.

[40]Brevard Childs, *The Book of Exodus* (Philadelphia: Westminster Press, 1974), 102, points out that this passage employs the concept of God's retributive justice. Pharaoh's son will die because God's son is kept in bondage. But this does not negate the use of this passage from its contribution to the theme of Israel's sonship.

[41]Albert Vanhoye, "L'oeuvre du Christ, don du Père (Jn 5, 36 et 17, 4)," *Recherches de Science Religieuse* 48 (1960):392.

[42]S. R. Driver, *A Critical and Exegetical Commentary on Deuteronomy*, third ed. (Edinburgh: T. & T. Clark, 1901), 352.

[43]Wolff, 197.

[44]Jeremias, 12.

admonishes Israel to "be holy for I am holy" (Lev. 11:44). Moses calls Israel's sonship into question not because of "disobedience," but because of their "defect" (Deut. 32:5). There is no defect in Yahweh, and he requires his "son" to manifest a like character.

This requirement to reflect the holiness of Yahweh stands behind his many commands to Israel. Because he is unique among the gods of the world, Israel is to be unique (Deut. 4:6-7). Their uniqueness among the nations is to be seen in shunning any form of idolatry (Deut. 13:6-11) and abstaining from sexual impurity (Deut. 22:22-30; 23:17-18). As Yahweh is a God of love and compassion (Deut. 4:37; 7:7, 8, etc.) so Israel is to show love to the stranger (Deut. 10:19; 24:17), the debtor (Deut. 15:1-3; 24:6, 10-11), the poor and servants (Deut. 15:4-18; 24:14-15), the widow and orphan (Deut. 14:29; 24:19-22), etc. The justice of Yahweh, evident in both the judgment of the guilty (Deut. 7:1-26) and fairness in that judgment (Deut. 10:17-18), is to be mirrored in Israel (Deut. 13:8; 13:12-14, respectively). Yahweh's faithfulness seen in bringing them out of Egypt as he promised (cf. Gen. 15:13-14), providing for them in the wilderness so they lacked nothing (Deut. 2:7) and his promise never to forget the covenant made with their fathers is to be reflected by Israel in their faithfulness to him apart from other gods (Deut. 6:14; 7:25-26), in their refraining from moving the geographical boundary markers (Deut. 19:14), and in their marriage relationships (Deut. 22:22-30).

One area of faithfulness worth noting is the concept of the first-born (Deut. 15:19-23). The first-born was to be consecrated (קָרַשׁ) to Yahweh, separated from the flock, and free from defect. Israel, too, was to be holy (קָדוֹשׁ) to Yahweh and separate from the rest of the world (Deut. 14:2), and thus was called to be blameless (Deut. 18:13). Yahweh's faithfulness and loving care for Israel was like the special treatment of a first-born. Israel was to respond to Yahweh as a first-born "son."

A very important theme in Israel's history which ties in with the father-son motif is that of "inheritance." This term is found repeatedly with reference to the land of Canaan and other promises Yahweh made to Israel (Exod. 15:17; Num. 16:14, etc.). As a faithful father provides for his son a portion of his wealth, so Yahweh provided for his son Israel.

Because of this likeness to Yahweh which Israel was to demonstrate, the nation was to be his representative-son. Israel's behavior should manifest to all the world that they are the unique people ("son") of the true God (Deut. 4:6-8). This is why Vriezen holds that the father-son terminology of the Old Testament expresses the *imago*

Dei.[45] As he states, "Man was originally created *in the image of God* [ital. his] . . . it denoted man in his peculiar relationship to God, in his vocation to be God's vice-regent on earth but most of all to reflect in his nature the nature of God, just as a child in the image of his father."[46]

Here then is an important purpose for the call to obedience. Israel, Yahweh's first-born son, is to obey the word of the LORD not merely for God's good pleasure but also that others might take notice of their righteous moral conduct. Such conduct will result in other peoples' recognition of and praise to the true God as they see the character of God evident in the character of Israel.[47]

In summary, the general picture of sonship to God in the Old Testament lies in the common ground shared by those referred to as God's "sons"--the angels and the nation of Israel. Both possess a functional sonship due to the act of obedience to God's commands. But their obedience stems from their sonship, not vice-versa. The aspect of sonship shared by both the angels and Israel is that they bear the image of God. For angels this follows *ipso facto* because God is their immediate creator and because they share his holiness.[48] But God also created (Isa. 43:1), begat (Deut. 32:18) and called the nation of Israel (Hos. 11:1), and thereby expected them to reflect his holiness (Lev. 11:1ff). Sonship for both angels and Israel is unconditional and is to be borne out in their functioning as God's represen-tatives. For the angels this meant representing God as his "messengers" (מַלְאָךְ, e.g. Gen 19:1, 15), as his "hosts" (צָבָא, e.g. Ps. 103:20-21 where the angels "perform his word"), and as his instruments of protection and ministry to his people (e.g. Exod. 23:20-22; Ps. 34:7; 2 Kings 19:35). Israel was to demonstrate that they were God's representatives by obeying his word. The resultant righteous behavior would reflect the image of their holy Father. By this the surrounding nations would see the character of the true and living God.

The Old Testament's more specific use of sonship to God is that applied to but one person within the nation of Israel. The meaning of sonship as it relates to the Messiah-king is the topic of study in the next section.

45Th. C. Vriezen, *An Outline of Old Testament Theology*, second ed. (Newton, MA: Charles T. Branford Co., 1970, 172.

46Ibid., 413.

47This may be the rationale for the use of the word עֵדָה ("witness, testimony") when speaking of the LORD's commandments to Israel (cf. Deut. 4:45; 6:17, 20). His commandments were meant to direct his covenant people in their conduct so that it might stand as a testimony to the character of the true God.

48Byrne, 13.

Unique Sonship: Israel's Messiah-king

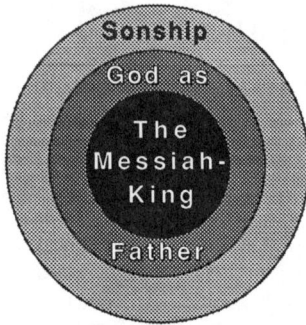

It is now necessary to establish the significance of sonship as applied to Israel's king. Not counting parallel passages, there are no less than four key references to the king as God's son (2 Sam. 7:14; 1 Chr. 22:10; Pss. 2:7; 89:26-27). Cooke says that in all probability, the concept of the king as God's son grew out of the soil of Israel as God's son.[49] Consequently, some sort of similarity must exist between the two ideas. Byrne sees the sonship of the king as "something very much domiciled within the general ideology of the people of God and a microcosm of the general Israelite 'sonship' motif."[50] This represents a further development in the concept of sonship, as God chooses one individual who will serve as his instrument.[51] Although God refers to his "begetting" the nation of Israel, only of the king are references found to God's "begetting" an individual. The king, the "anointed one" or messiah, is therefore God's "son" in a more unique sense.[52]

The fact that both the nation of Israel and the king of Israel are called "son" points up one of the problems of the study. As with the nation Israel, the sonship of Israel's king is not a unique idea in the ancient Near East. Most monarchs were considered "sons" of the national deities.[53]

Writers such as Martin Noth see the office of the Israelite king as a purely secular institution occupied by an ordinary man.[54] But some see Israel's concept of the king as identical with the divine kingship of other cultures in the ancient Near East. As Mowinckel puts it,

---

[49]Cooke, "The Israelite King as Son of God," 217.

[50]Byrne, 18.

[51]D. Wayne Montgomery, "Concepts of Divine Kingship in the Ancient Near East: The Messiah Yahweh as God's Son"(Th.D. dissertation, The Iliff School of Theology, 1969), 215-16.

[52]Paul Heinisch, *Theology of the Old Testament*, trans. William G. Heidt (Collegeville, MN: The Order of St. Benedict, Inc., 1955), 347.

[53]Sigmund Mowinckel, "General Oriental and Specific Israelite Elements in the Israelite Conception of the Sacral Kingdom," in *The Sacral Kingship*, ed. Georg Widengren et. al. (Leiden: E. J. Brill, 1959), 284.

[54]Martin Noth, "Gott, König, Volk im Alten Testament," in *Gesammelte Studien zum Alten Testament* (München: Chr. Kaiser Verlag, 1960), 188-229.

The idea about the king is fundamentally the same [in Israel] as in the rest of the ancient East . . . the most important elements of the ancient Oriental's view of the king are as follows: the king was more or less clearly and consistently looked upon as 'divine.' In Egypt he was held to be a god incarnate begotten by the god. . . . In Mesopotamia and Asia Minor the king is a man made divine, chosen for the kingship by the gods.[55]

The position articulated by Mowinckel is termed the "General Pattern Theory" because adherents claim to see a pattern in the ancient Near East with respect to an ideology centering on the king.[56] This ideology supposedly saw the sonship of the king as the ideal embodiment of the national deity.[57] Or, as Mowinckel puts it, "Volksgott ist König."[58]

Based on the assertions of the "General Pattern" school, Montgomery offers a definition of divine kingship,

Divine kingship is a belief or ideology which ascribes divinity to the ruling personage: the king partakes of, and participates in the divine as opposed to or as exceeding the human sphere of reality. . . . It is to assert that the king in some fundamental and essential way is considered to be potentially . . . identical with the deity.[59]

But as Henri Frankfort points out, the term "divine kingship" is in actuality ambiguous.[60] The problem lies in the divergence of views when the various cultures are compared.

Textual evidence shows that the Egyptian pharaoh was considered divine, an embodiment of a god.[61] S. A. B. Mercer says, "The Egyptian approached his king as he would a god . . . the Egyptian

---

[55]Sigmund Mowinckel, 283.

[56]See the standard work on this position, Ivan Engnell, *Studies in the Divine Kingship in the Ancient Near East* (Uppsala: Almquist & Wiksells Boktryckeri A.-B., 1943),

[57]Montgomery, 9.

[58]Sigmund Mowinckel, *Psalmenstudien* (Amsterdam: Verlag P. Schippers, 1961), 1:2, 39.

[59]Montgomery, 2-3.

[60]Henri Frankfort, *The Problem of Similarity in Ancient Near Eastern Religion* (London: Oxford University Press, 1951), 3.

[61]*Ancient Near Eastern Texts Relating to the Old Testament*, third ed., ed. James B. Pritchard, 11, 21, 205-15, 234.

really believed that the Pharaoh was an incarnate god."[62] E. O. James adds, ". . . the pharaoh [was] in fact the gods he embodied in their various manifestations and syncretisms."[63]

The situation in Mesopotamia is different, however. Although kings in this land frequently referred to themselves as gods in a titular sense, they were never worshiped as deity in the manner of the pharaohs.[64] James says,

> Although in Mesopotamia the monarch appears to have been regarded as a divine institution in origin and each occupant of the "local throne" was thought to have been selected by the gods through the necessary omens. . . . these claims did not constitute actual deification. This status was believed to have come to an end once and for all when the heroic age ceased with the Isin Dynasty (c. 2072 B. C.).[65]

Although the Ras Shamra texts of Canaan are not as clear about the king's divinity as those of Egypt, the evidence from other cultures demonstrates that the "General Pattern Theory" goes too far. Not every culture in the ancient Near East saw the king as divine. De Vaux summarizes his findings,

> In ancient Egypt the king was revered as god, but in Mesopotamia only in the early days was the king supposed to possess a divine character. Babylonia and Assyria indicate that although the king held certain supernatural power, he still remained a man among men. The Hittites deified kings only after their death, and in Palestine and Syria limited evidence does not warrant the conclusion that kings were deified. . . . it is not true to say that the idea of a divine king was shared by all people of the ancient Near East.[66]

In this vein Cooke says,

> The existence of a uniform conception of the king's divine nature and status in the ancient Near East cannot be demonstrated. The author's [Cooke's] own study of relevant texts has shown the inaccuracy of sweeping general statements. Only in Egyptian

[62]S. A. B. Mercer, *The Religion of Ancient Egypt* (Luzac & Co., Ltd., 1949), 252.

[63]E. O. James, *The Ancient Gods* (New York: G. P. Putnam's Sons, 1960), 15.

[64]Montgomery, 26.

[65]James, 120.

[66]Roland de Vaux, *Ancient Israel, Its Life and Institution*, trans. John McHugh (New York: McGraw Hill Book Co., 1961), 111-112.

texts does the unqualified divine sonship of the ruler regularly appear.[67]

With specific reference to Israel's king de Vaux says,

> Israel's religion, indeed with its faith in Yahweh as a personal God, unique and transcendent, made any deification of the king impossible. The prophets witness to the same, since although they accuse the kings of many crimes, never is mention made of claiming divinity. Israel never had, never could have had, any idea of a king who was a god.[68]

Yet Israel's king, like monarchs of surrounding cultures, is sometimes called God's "son." In what sense is this so? A. R. Johnson argues that it is not that the king experiences a metaphorical transformation so that he becomes divine, but that he is the object of Yahweh's special favor.[69] Speaking of Israel's king, another writer says,

> Sonship of the king relates to the function and office . . . rather than to the transformation of his nature. As son the king becomes God's representative, ruling according to God's desire and in his power.[70]

Gerhard von Rad points out that, unlike any other king in the ancient Orient, Israel's king and Israel's God were related by the king's possession of God's Spirit.[71]

Some see this relationship best expressed by the term "adoption." Of Ps. 2:7 Weiser says,

> It is understandable that the Old Testament rejected the idea of the physical sonship of the king. . . . In fact, the psalmist, too, excludes the idea of a physical begetting by adding the word "today" and by using the ancient formula of adoption "you are my son," though he leaves untouched the formula "I have begotten

---

[67]Cooke, "The Israelite King as Son of God," 208.

[68]de Vaux, 113.

[69]Aubrey R. Johnson, *Sacral Kingship in Ancient Israel* (Cardiff: University of Wales Press, 1967), 25.

[70]James Robert Edwards, "The Son of God: Its Antecedents in Judaism and Hellenism and Its Use in the Earliest Gospel" (Ph.D. dissertation, Fuller Theological Seminary, 1978), 13.

[71]Gerhard von Rad, *Old Testament Theology*, trans. D. M. G. Stalker (New York: Harper & Row, 1962), 1:323.

you." . . . [but] he transforms that alien idea into the idea of adoption, that is to say, into the declaration of the sonship of the king that took place on the day of his enthronement.[72]

The difficulty in this position is the absence of the idea of adoption in the Old Testament. According to Haag, "It is incorrect to interpret this expression as a kind of adoption of the king by Yahweh" because the institution of adoption was not known in Israel.[73] Cooke points out, however, that "Even though the Old Testament evidence for adoption in the strict sense is extremely meager, [yet] a relationship was known to the Hebrews which was for all practical purposes concerning the parties involved an adoptive relationship."[74] That is to say, the Old Testament will not allow a literal sonship for the king, yet God calls him "son." And because that sonship occurs at a point in time ("today I have begotten you"), the concept of adoption--though not prevalent in Israel's culture--is the best approximation.

Twentieth century western civilization struggles with the terminology and meaning of the king as God's "son." But for the Hebrew there was apparently no difficulty. As mentioned above, the king's sonship is but a microcosm of the general Israelite sonship motif. Fohrer elaborates on this when he says, "As the election of Israel and God's assurances to it in the events of the exodus and Sinai constitute the form and basis of the idea of the election of David and his house and of the so-called Davidic covenant, so the concept of Israel's sonship is well-adapted to serve as a model for the relation between Yahweh and the Davidic dynasty."[75]

But as we noted in our examination of Israel's sonship, the issue of obedience played a key role. Edwards is correct in pointing out that the Davidic covenant, like the Abrahamic, is unconditional.[76] But as Weiser notes, the importance of the function of the king (and thus for the sonship of the king) is that he is God's *appointed* one to carry out his divine will.[77] Therefore, obedience is an important aspect in the sonship of the king as it is for the sonship of Israel. And although God's covenant with David was unconditional, this assured only that David's throne would endure forever, not that it would be perpetually occupied. Psalm 132:12 articulates this conditional aspect.

Interestingly, not only is the term "son" not applied to every king,

---

[72]Artur Weiser, *The Psalms*, trans. Herbert Hartwell (Philadelphia: The Westminster Press, 1962), 113.

[73]H. Haag, "בן," 155.

[74]Cooke, "The Israelite King as Son of God," 215-16.

[75]Fohrer, 351.

[76]Edwards, 2-3, n. 7.

[77]Weiser, 113.

it may have been applied only to David and Solomon. More specifically, it cannot be stated dogmatically that any king besides Solomon, alone, was referred to as God's "son." This is evident when the sonship texts are examined. The reference in 2 Sam. 7:14 (par. 1 Chr. 17:13) is obviously to David's son, later identified as Solomon (1 Chr. 22:9). Psalm 89 is not a Davidic psalm, but is attributed to Ethan who refers back to the LORD's promises to David in 2 Sam. 7.[78] Psalm 2 is anonymous, and for this reason Delitzsch says it cannot be considered Davidic.[79] The only sonship passage that remains is 1 Chr. 22:10. Here a clear reference is made to Solomon as God's "son." Thus the only certain referent with respect to sonship is Solomon.[80]

It is also noteworthy that Yahweh, himself, gives Solomon his name even before he is born. The name thus seems to be connected with the concept of sonship, for they both proceed from the LORD in the same context. Yahweh gives a brief explanation for the name, saying he shall be Solomon (שְׁלֹמֹה) because God will give him peace (שָׁלוֹם) during his reign.

The word "peace" (שָׁלוֹם) means more than the absence of strife. The Old Testament employs the word to mean "completeness, soundness, wholeness, health, prosperity."[81] Von Rad says, "at root it means 'well-being.'"[82] Such was the ideal for the ruler in the ancient world. Wolfgang Roth says,

> Behind the notion that the king brings and guarantees peace is the so-called ancient Near East royal ideology. There peace is understood not so much as the opposite of war as . . . justice and

---

[78]Ibid., 590-91.

[79]Franz Delitzsch, *Biblical Commentary on the Psalms*, trans. Francis Bolton, reprint ed. (Grand Rapids: William B. Eerdmans, 1949), 1:89. In Acts 4:25 Peter attributes Psalm 2 to David. However this ascription may be similar to Matthew's attributing the words of Zechariah to Jeremiah in Matt. 27:9. Matthew does this because Jeremiah was first in the group of prophetic books. Gundry calls this a "Jewish practice [of] composite quotations" (*Matthew*. A Commentary on His Literary and Theological Art (Grand Rapids: William B. Eerdmans, 1982), 557). Peter may have linked the Psalm to David since he was the premier author of the Psalms (Weiser, 94-95).

[80]Note also how both "his kingdom" (Solomon's) and "your kingdom" (David's) are used interchangeably in these passages. Thus, although David may seem to have some part in the concept of sonship, this is only because it is his offspring who is called God's "son." David's throne, therefore, becomes the throne of God's "son."

[81]Francis Brown, S. R. Driver, and Charles A. Briggs, *A Hebrew and English Lexicon of the Old Testament*, s.v. "שָׁלוֹם," 1022-23.

[82]*Theological Dictionary of the New Testament*, s.v. "εἰρήνη," by Gerhard von Rad, 2 (1969):402.

harmony. . . . Through his rule the king upholds this order.[83]

This was true because, as Henri Frankfort explains,

> The ancient Near East considered kingship the very basis of civilization. . . . Security, peace and justice could not prevail without a ruler to champion them. . . . Whatever was significant was imbedded in the life of the cosmos, and it was precisely the king's function to maintain the harmony of that integration.[84]

But even more important for the present study, J. Maxwell Miller points out that the monarch in the ancient Orient had the above-mentioned responsibility because he was the "image" of God. Just as God at creation had bestowed upon man (who was his image) the responsibility to care for the creation, so he held the king (who is his image) responsible for the care of the people.[85]

Thus Israel's king was to provide well-being for God's people. This was because as Israel's "father," God had promised to care for them as a father cares for his son (cf. Deut. 1:31). A. R. Johnson observes. ". . . [that] the king held office as Yahweh's agent or vice-gerent is shown quite clearly in the rite of anointing which marked him out as a sacral person endowed with such special responsibility for the well-being of his people."[86]

Well-being for Israel was indeed maintained during Solomon's reign. Of this period Bright says, "Israel enjoyed a security and a material plenty such as she had never dreamed of before and was never to know again."[87] But as the biblical account shows, that harmony lasted only as long as Solomon's heartbeat. In the wake of his death, the strife that followed began at the throne, itself (1 Kings 12:1-20, par.). No king thereafter was ever referred to as God's "son." Instead, as in Ps. 89, they looked back to Yahweh's promise to David.

Fohrer holds that the reason Yahweh declares an individual the legitimate king by calling him "son" is not merely because he is in the

---

[83]Wolfgang Roth, "The Language of Peace: Shalom and Eirene," *Explor* 3 (1977):71.

[84]Henri Frankfort, *Kingship and the Gods* (Chicago: University of Chicago Press, 1948), 3.

[85]J. Maxwell Miller, "In the 'Image' and 'Likeness' of God," *Journal of Biblical Literature* 91 (1972):294-96.

[86]R. Johnson, "Hebrew Conceptions of Kingship," in *Myth, Ritual and Kingship*, ed. Samuel Henry Hooke (Oxford: Clarendon Press, 1958), 207-08.

[87]John Bright, *A History of Israel*, third ed. (Philadelphia: The Westminster Press, 1981), 212.

Davidic line, but because God chooses to share his rule with him.[88]
Thus a descendent of David may sit on Israel's throne, but only the
one chosen by God can be his "son"--"highest of the kings of the earth"
(Ps. 89:27). Throughout their history, as Ps. 89 testifies, the people of
Israel longed for one to fulfill the promise made to David.[89]

To this point it has been shown that sonship for Israel's king
meant: 1) he was the designated ruler because he was uniquely
chosen by God and 2) he was to demonstrate obedience by functioning
in God's will.[90] David and especially Solomon met the first criterion
while both failed the second. But we have also seen the intimation of a
third aspect.

As with Israel's sonship, obedience for the king is but the necessary consequence of being called as God's representative. This is the
reason for the debate concerning divine kingship. As Kidding notes,
the deity and the king in the ancient Near East are inseparably bound
together, so that when the king acts, it is the god's act.[91] Mowinckel
says,

> The king's power and legitimacy is [sic] supported by the theory
> that he is the divine representative of the god, called and en-
> throned by him, and given authority as his deputy among men.
> The king is thus the representative of the gods on earth, the
> steward of the god or the gods.[92]

This principle is evident for Israel's king in Ps. 89:21, 23, and 25.
Whatever is said of the king here issues from the world-encompas-
sing power of Yahweh, himself.[93] The earthly reign of the king is
intended to reflect the heavenly reign of God, for the king is God's
representative to the people.[94]

---

[88]Fohrer, 350.

[89]Obviously the lines of Ps. 89:19-29 are not to be taken to refer to David,
exclusively. As Aubrey Johnson says, "They must be read in light of what we know
about Israelite ideas of corporate personality. . . . the line of David is to issue in one
who shall be something more than 'the Messiah of Yahweh.' He . . . will be the
accepted 'son' of the national deity . . ." *Sacral Kingship in Ancient Israel*, 27-28.

[90]Ibid., 143; Weiser, 113.

[91]K. A. H. Kidding, "The High God and the King as Symbols of Totality," in
The Sacral Kingship, 54.

[92]Mowinckel, "General Oriental and Specific Israelite Elements in the Israelite Conception of the Sacral Kingdom," 283-84.

[93]Cf. Hans-Joachim Kraus, *Psalmen* (Neukirchen-Vluyn: Neukirchener
Verlag, 1978), 2:790-91.

[94]Walther Eichrodt, *Theology of the Old Testament*, trans. J. A. Baker (Philadelphia: Westminster Press, 1961), 1:163.

As God's representative, however, his "son" functioned as more than just a ruler. James notes that in Israel, the king, priest and prophet were inseparably bound together.[95] This is especially evident in the cases of Saul, David, and Solomon who respectively offered sacrifices (1 Sam. 13:9; 2 Sam. 6:17-18; 2 Chr. 1:6), and prophesied (1 Sam. 10:10; David and Solomon's volume of wisdom literature). Moreover, the priesthood of God's chosen king is made evident in Ps. 110:4 ("a priest forever according to the order of Melchizedek"). But whereas the priestly functions of David and Solomon pleased the LORD (2 Sam. 24:25; 2 Chr. 7:1-3), Saul's did not (1 Sam. 13:13-14). Moreover, there is no evidence that, as with the term "son," any king following Solomon ever functioned as a priest.[96] Thus only David and Solomon served God by functioning as prophet, priest, and king.

These three offices find common ground in the function of "representatives" or "mediators." The prophet is obviously a representative and mediator for God, functioning as God's "speaking tube."[97] The priest, too, can be seen as a representative and mediator. Sabourin says, "In his different functions the Israelite priest was a mediator: as oracular consultant and as a teacher of the Torah he represented God before men; as a minister before the altar he represented men before God."[98] De Vaux agrees saying, "The priest was a mediator, like the king and prophet."[99] Basically, then, it is precisely *because* the chosen king-"son" is a representative for God that he can also function as prophet and priest.[100]

Therefore, according to evidence from both the surrounding cultures and the Old Testament, the Israelite king was not considered to be divine. But as God's "son" he was a chosen representative to function as God's vice-regent. He stood as the representative-mediator, who not only held the office of king, but functioned as a prophet and a priest. In his acts, the acts of God were to be evident. The relationship between Yahweh and his "son" the king was such that,

> Accordingly it should be no matter for surprize that the king's person was regarded by the pious followers as sacrosanct. . . . Indeed the very cursing of the king was something to be

---

[95] E O. James, "The Sacral Kingship and the Priesthood," in *The Sacral Kingship*, 68.

[96] Cf. Uzziah's attempt to burn incense and the Yahweh's resultant judgment, 2 Chr. 26:16-21.

[97] Eichrodt, 1:340.

[98] Leopold Sabourin, *Priesthood: A Comparative Study* (Leiden: E. J. Brill, 1973), 101.

[99] de Vaux, 357.

[100] Vriezen, 368.

condemned in the same breath as the cursing of Yahweh himself (Exod. 22:28; 1 Kings 21:10, 13).[101]

One more issue must be addressed before summarizing sonship in the Old Testament. The question of divine kingship for the Israelite monarch exists not only because of the "inextricable bond" between the two.[102] This question is also raised because certain passages of Scripture seem to indicate the Messiah's divinity.

In referring to the sonship of Messiah, Ps. 2:7 uses the formula, "I have begotten you" (יְלִדְתִּיךָ) This is similar to the formula employed in Ps. 110:3 (יְלִדְתִּיךָ) which Cooke also translates "I have begotten you."[103] The question is, to whom is the psalmist referring? Yahweh is obviously speaking (v. 1), but David the king refers to someone else who is his "lord" (אֲדֹנִי). Is the referent divine or human?

An even greater difficulty is encountered in Psalm 45. Here the psalmist is addressing the king on the occasion of his wedding.[104] Verse six proclaims, "Your throne, O God, is forever and ever." Rogerson says by understatement, "There has been much discussion about how to translate this phrase."[105] Though various translations have been offered, that which shows the king being addressed as "God" (אֱלֹהִים) prevails. This is the translation preferred by ancient versions.[106] Moreover as Albrektson says, one cannot avoid this "straight-forward translation."[107]

The tension which exists in this verse is that of avoiding divine kingship. Translators and commentators are reticent to call the king "God," for the Old Testament nowhere else expresses divine kingship. And, as Perowne says, "It is impossible to suppose the mystery of the Incarnation was distinctly revealed, and clearly understood, under the Old Testament dispensation."[108]

The resolution for the Old Testament saint probably came in seeing that the term אֱלֹהִים was applied to men in other places in the Old Testament (cf. Exod. 7:1; 21:6; 22:8, 9). Men who were so-called

[101]Johnson, "Hebrew Conceptions of Kingship," 208-209.

[102]Montgomery, 172.

[103]Cooke, "The Israelite King as Son of God," 222.

[104]Weiser, 362.

[105]J. W. Rogerson and J. W. McKay, *Psalms 1-50* (Cambridge: University Press, 1977), 215.

[106]A. A. Anderson, *The Book of Psalms* (Grand Rapids: William B. Eerdmans, 1981), 1:349.

[107]Bertil Albrektson, *History and the Gods* (Lund, Sweden: GWK Gleerup, 1967), 51, n. 46.

[108]J. J. Stewart Perowne, *The Book of Psalms* (London: George Bell and Sons, 1878), 381.

were viewed as God's righteous representatives.[109] Nonetheless, the use of אֱלֹהִים with reference to the king leaves room for the literal interpretation, especially in light of the next verse. Here the same term is used with obvious reference to Yahweh ("therefore God, your God, has anointed you").

Summary of the Old Testament Background

The examination of the concept of sonship has surfaced several facets of usage. Beginning with "sonship" in general, the term was seen to connote a relationship or association at varying degrees, ranging from a loose and general "association with," to that which expresses the "sharing of a nature or quality." Sometimes, as in the literal usage, sonship carries the idea of "reflecting the character or image" of the father.

These meanings carried over into the examination of sonship to God. Angels are "sons of God" because they bear his image and obey him by doing his handiwork. Although the individual Israelite could not claim God as his direct progenitor, still God says he "begat" the nation as his first-born. And just as the angels, they were to demonstrate sonship by obedience. In so doing, their character before the rest of the world would reflect the character of their Father. By this the world would know the character of the one true God.

The kingship of Israel was a microcosm of the representative nature of the nation. As the nation of Israel was "first-born" (highest in God's esteem) among the nations of the earth, so the king was the "first-born, highest of the kings of the earth" (Ps. 89:27).[110] In the same way in which Yahweh had called the people of Israel his "son" even before they are considered a nation (Exod. 4:22), so he calls David's offspring his "son" even before he is born (1 Chr. 22:9-10). Just as the nation of Israel was God's "son" in serving a priestly function for God among the nations (Exod. 19:6), so the king as "son" also functioned as a priest for the nation of Israel. Paralleling the prophetic function of Israel who was to "proclaim peace to the nations" (Deut. 20:10), the king proclaimed God's word in poetic literature.

Thus both Israel and the chosen king are called God's "son" to function as his representatives--called to represent him before others and to function in obedience. If obedience was lacking, then God's image was lacking, and sonship was tainted. While God would never

---

109Weiser, 363. Cf. Allen P. Ross, "Psalms," in *The Bible Knowledge Commentary.* Old Testament Edition, 827.

110*Theological Dictionary of the Old Testament*, s.v. "בְּכוֹר," by M. Tsevat, 2:126.

break his covenant with Israel, their sonship was repeatedly questioned. This was not a question of the Father's faithfulness, but of his son's. The sonship of the king was not merely called into question. Although the covenant with David was eternally binding, the sonship of the king was non-existent in the Old Testament after Solomon.

Because of this disobedience, the absence of the demonstration of sonship and the tainting of God's image, both God and Israel longed for the day when true sonship could be realized.[111] God desired one who would reflect his character before men. Israel hoped for one who would not exhibit the frailties of even their greatest kings. This is reflected in Old Testament writings such as the Second Psalm. As one writer says, this psalm "paints a picture of a dominion of the king which not even Israel's greatest kings--David, Solomon, or Josiah--possessed."[112] Such was the hope of the Jewish people at the appearing of Jesus of Nazareth.

---

[111]Cooke, "The Israelite King as Son of God," 225-26.
[112]Edwards, 17.

3

The "Son of God" Title
in the New Testament

The purpose of this chapter is to examine how the sonship of God
from the Old Testament might be applied to Jesus. Does the "Son of
God" have Messianic implications, and *only* Messianic implications?
If the title does stem from Old Testament roots, can there be any
implications for Jesus' deity? This is a necessary question since one
of the reasons Bultmann postulated his "transference theory" was his
contention that the Early Church did not see the "Son of God" as a
supernatural being. He says, ". . . it is clear that neither in Judaism
nor in the [early] Christian Church could this title have the
mythological meaning it later had in Hellenistic Christianity; that is,
it did not designate the Messiah as a supernatural being begotten by
God, but was simply a royal title."[1]

As in the previous chapter, this examination of "sonship" might
be visualized as three concentric circles. However, the New Testament examination of the title will proceed in the reverse order of the
Old Testament examination. Rather than starting with the meaning
of "sonship," and ending with Messiahship, the examination will
commence with the innermost circle, i.e. Messiahship, and proceed
outward through Christ's filial relationship with God, concluding
with a discussion of the fuller meaning of Christ's sonship.

Jesus the Son of God:
the unique Messiah-King

By the time Jesus' public ministry began, the person and work of the
Messiah had been a subject of speculation for hundreds of years. The
term "Messiah" had come to be something of a *terminus technicus* by
the first century B.C. for the Anointed One who would be God's deliv-

---

[1]Rudolf Bultmann, *Theology of the New Testament*, trans. Kendrick Grobel
(New York: Charles Scribner's Sons, 1951), 1:50.

erer in the days of eschatological consummation.[2] Referring to Ps. Sol. chs. 17-18 and 1QS 9:11, Longenecker says, "What seems to have captured the peoples' fancy was that the Messiah would be a political and nationalistic ruler--even a military leader."[3] But parallel with this ran the belief that the Messiah would be one who would bring good news and wellbeing for the people according to Isa. 52:7.[4]

The question is, what part did the title "Son of God" play? Although the Old Testament holds the concept of "sonship" for both Israel and the king, neither is properly called "son of God." This led some commentators to deny that the title could have been used for the Messiah at the time of Jesus. Fitzmyer is cautious in making any direct connection.[5] Kümmel holds there is no sure evidence that pre-Christian Judaism held the title "son of God" to be specifically Messianic.[6]

Part of the problem, of course, is the reticence of intertestamental writers to employ the title "Son of God." This was to avoid any linking of the divine kingship prevalent in the ancient Orient.[7] But recent evidence goes contrary to Kümmel's assertion.

The anticipated Messiah clearly was linked to texts that referred to him as God's "son."[8] As Moule says, "It is certainly demonstrable that, to be God's son was . . . recognized as one of the Messiah's characteristics."[9] Fitzmyer says that some passages in Qumran texts

---

[2]Richard N. Longenecker, *The Christology of Early Jewish Christianity* (Naperville, IL: Alec R. Allenson, Inc., 1970), 64-66.

[3]Ibid., 66.

[4]Joseph A. Fitzmyer, "Further Light on Melchizedek from Qumran Cave 11," *Journal of Biblical Literature* 86 (1967):40.

[5]Idem, *A Wandering Aramean* (Missoula, MT: Scholar's Press, 1979), 105-106.

[6]Werner Georg Kümmel, *Die Theologie des Neuen Testaments nach seinem Hauptzeugen: Jesus, Paulus, Johannes* (Göttingen: Vandenhoeck & Ruprecht, 1969), 67-68.

[7]*Theological Dictionary of the New Testament* s.v. "υἱός," by Eduard Lohse, 360.

[8]Longenecker, 95.

[9]C. F. D. Moule, *The Origin of Christology* (Cambridge: Cambridge University Press, 1959), 28.

are strikingly similar to those applied to Jesus in the New Testament.[10] One text to which he refers is from 4Q 243. It reads, "But your son shall be great upon the earth, O king . . . he shall be called son of the Great God . . . he shall be hailed as the Son of God and they shall call him Son of the Most High . . ." which is reminiscent of Lk. 1:32, "He shall be called the Son of the Most High . . ."

In light of such texts, it would have been viewed as blasphemous for a powerless person to call himself the Messiah, for as such he was also "Son of the Blessed" and representative of God.[11] Matthew Black contends the evidence from Qumran makes it "fully certain" that the "son" titles in the Davidic strand of pre-Christian Messianism stand behind the Christological concept of the "Son."[12] Howard Kee sees the title "Son of God" as one of the ways the Jews designated the redemptive figure of the end-time.[13] As Reginald Fuller says, "Son of God was just coming into use as a Messianic title in pre-Christian Judaism."[14] James Dunn adds, "Whereas it earlier appeared that 'Son of God' had no messianic significance within the Judaism of Jesus' time, the evidence from the Dead Sea Scrolls now begins to point in the other direction."[15]

But at what point is Jesus viewed as Messiah and Son of God? Paul says Jesus was "descended from the seed of David, designated the Son of God by the resurrection" (Rom. 1:3-4). But Jeremias states that, "Faith in the resurrection of a murdered messenger of God certainly does not amount to belief in his Messiahship."[16] Dahl contends that the resurrection of Jesus alone could not have confirmed him as Messiah and thus he must have been viewed as such before this event.[17] The seeds of the various Christological titles of the Ear-ly Church, including that of "Son of God," must be seen to be a part of

---

[10]Joseph Fitzmyer, "The Contribution of Qumran Aramaic to the Study of the New Testament," *New Testament Studies* 20 (1973-74):394.

[11]Otto Betz, *What Do We Know about Jesus?* (Philadelphia: The Westminster Press, 1968), 89.

[12]Matthew Black, "The Christological Use of the Old Testament in the New Testament," *New Testament Studies* 18 (1971-72):2-4.

[13]Howard C. Kee, *Community of the New Age* (Philadelphia: The Westminster Press, 1977), 122.

[14]Reginald H. Fuller, *The Foundation of New Testament Christology* (New York: Charles Scribner's Sons, 1965), 32.

[15]James D. G. Dunn, *Unity and Diversity in the New Testament* (London: SCM Press, Ltd., 1977), 45.

[16]Joachim Jeremias, *New Testament Theology*, trans. John Bowden (New York: Charles Scribner's Son, 1971), 1:255.

[17]Nils Alstrup Dahl, "The Crucified Messiah," in *The Crucified Messiah and Other Essays* (Minneapolis, MN: Augsburg Publishing House, 1974), 23-36.

Jesus' life before the Easter event, says Kim.[18] As Marshall states, "The Resurrection confirms and manifests an [already] existing position."[19] Vielhauer sees the title as necesarily applied even before the pronouncement of the centurion at the cross (Mk. 15:39).[20]

The manifestation of Jesus as Messiah and Son of God goes back to his baptism,[21] which parallels the "anointing" of the Old Testament king.[22] Indeed, the wording of the voice from heaven is reminiscent of Ps. 2:7.[23] As Davey says, from the time of his baptism, "The evidence of the Synoptics is that Christ regarded himself as Messiah and therefore the Son of God."[24]

But some see the designation "Messiah" as an inaccurate title for Jesus during his life because of its political connotation.[25] Yet Donahue says, "The 4Q Qumran text where a royal figure is addressed in an apocalyptic context as Son of God as well as the mixture of political and religious ideology in the Zealot movement indicate [sic] that a distinction between 'religious' and 'political' is not applicable to first century Judaism."[26] Jesus certainly saw himself in a Messianic role. As McDermott points out, Jesus not only accepts Peter's confession of him as Messiah (Mk. 8:29) but he never rejected any Messianic title.[27]

Kingsbury shows these Messianic titles include "King of the

---

[18]Seyoon Kim, *The Origin of Paul's Gospel* (Tübingen: J. C. B. Mohr (Paul Siebeck), 1981), 106, n. 1.

[19]I. Howard Marshall, "The Divine Sonship of Jesus," *Interpretation* 21 (1967):102.

[20]Philip Vielhauer, "Erwägungen zum Christologie des Markusevangeliums," in *Aufsätze zum Neues Testaments* (München: Chr. Kaiser Verlag, 1965), 212-14. 20

[21]Barnabas Lindars, *New Testament Apologetic* (London: SCM Press, Ltd., 1961), 111.

[22]I. Howard Marshall, "Son of God or Servant of Yahweh?--A Reconsideration of Mark 1.11," *New Testament Studies* 15 (1968-69):329.

[23]*Theological Dictionary of the New Testament*, s.v. "υἱός," by Eduard Schweizer, 8:368.

[24]Ernest Davey, *The Jesus of St. John: Historical and Christological Studies in the Fourth Gospel* (London: Lutterworth Press, 1958), 136.

[25]E.g., T. Alec Burkill, *Mysterious Revelation* (Ithaca, NY: Cornell University Press, 1963), 152; Walter Grundmann, *Das Evangelium nach Markus* (Berlin: Evangelische Verlangsanstalt, 1984),168; Dennis E. Nineham, *The Gospel of St. Mark* (Harmondsworth, Middlesex: Penguin Books, 1963), 224-25.

[26]John R. Donahue, "Temple, Trial, and Royal Christology (Mark 14:53-65)," in *The Passion in Mark*, ed. W. H. Kelber (Philadelphia: Fortress Press, 1976), 74-75.

[27]John M. McDermott, "Jesus and the Son of God Title," *Gregorianum* 62:2 (1981):305.

Jews," "Son of David," and "Son of God."[28] That the titles "Son of God" and "Messiah" were seen to be practically synonymous is evident from Peter's confession (Matt. 16:16 par), Caiaphas' question (Matt. 26:63 par), the demoniac's confession (Lk. 4:41), Martha's affirmation (Jn. 11:27;), John's statement of purpose for his Gospel (Jn. 20:31), and Paul's initial preaching of Jesus (Acts 9:20-22). These examples, plus the fact that Jesus never rebuked those who used Messianic titles, seem to oppose van Iersel's contention that Jesus hardly ever used the title to refer to himself.[29] But even so, as Lohse asserts, the theological correctness of the designation does not depend on Jesus' using it.[30]

The affirmation of Jesus as Messiah comes from more than the passages cited above, however. As Kingsbury says, the surest evidence that "Son of God" defines "Messiah" comes from the use of the former title by God, himself, at Jesus' baptism and tranfiguration.[31] On both occasions God's voice confirms the use of "Messiah" in the context of the passage.

Thus the transfiguration also points to Jesus' Messiahship. Kee notes that the admonition "Listen to him" is an allusion to Deut. 18:15 where some Qumran texts understood the "prophet" to be the eschatological figure who would reveal the truth of God to Israel.[32] Goppelt says of the transfiguration,

> The ideas that were commonly accepted at the time indicate that the disciples must have interpreted the presence of these two men [Moses and Elijah] as a proclamation that the new age had come. This also explains Peter's mysterious remark about the erection of shelters, because in the last days God will again pitch his tent among his people, just as he did in the time of Moses. Moreover, the cloud that enveloped them had appeared during the wilderness wandering at the dedication of the first temple as a sign of God's presence, and it was expected that it would reappear in the last days.[33]

---

[28]Jack Dean Kingsbury, *The Christology of Mark's Gospel* (Philadelphia: Fortress Press, 1983), 55.

[29]B. M. F. van Iersel, *'Der Sohn' in den Synoptischen Jesusworten* (Leiden: E. J. Brill, 1964), 26. But notice Jesus' undeniable use of the title for himself in Jn. 10:36.

[30]*Theological Dictionary of the New Testament*, s.v. "υἱός," by Eduard Lohse, 8:366.

[31]Kingsbury, 98.

[32]Howard Kee, *Community of the New Age*, 123.

[33]Leonard Goppelt, *Typos: The Typological Interpretation of the Old Testament in the New*, trans. Donald H. Madvig (Grand Rapids: William B. Eerd-

Two of the major events in Jesus' ministry, therefore, show him to be the Son of God in the Old Testament tradition. But what about his death and resurrection? The subject of his death will be addressed later. Suffice it at this point to say that intertestamental literature sometimes viewed the suffering and pious individual as God's "son" (cf. Wis. Sol. 2:12-20; 4:10, 13-15; 5:1-5; Sir. 4:10). Edwards says, "Son of God is depicted in intertestamental literature as the suffering righteous man who is humiliated and only later exalted."[34]

But is the resurrection of Jesus drawn from the Old Testament? Paul says Jesus was declared the "Son of God with power" at this event (Rom. 1:4). But Paul's statement is not without some Old Testament connection, for in verse three he says, "concerning his Son, who was born of the seed of David." Van Iersel points out that the key words here, σπέρμα, υἱός, and ἀνάστασις also occur in 2 Sam. 7:12-14 of the Septuagint.[35]

The key passage which generates debate on this question is Acts 13:33 where Paul says, "that God has raised up Jesus as it is also written in the Second Psalm, 'You are My Son, today I have begotten You.'" The question concerns the word "raised up" (ἀνίστημι). F. F. Bruce says the word does not refer to the resurrection but only to the promise of "raising up" the Messiah among the people.[36] Everett Harrison says it is "dubious" to apply this verse to the resurrection.[37]

But some commentators disagree with the former position. Marshall and Byrne hold that the weight of the argument goes to Acts 13:33 being a reference to the resurrection because of intertestamental literature.[38] Marshall refers to Wis. chapters 2-3 where the righteous man is vindicated as God's "son" because God delivers him from his adversaries.[39] Schweizer says it is "obvious" and "clear" that ἀνίστημι refers to the resurrection because "the context deals with the death and resurrection of Christ, and the following verse (v. 34) uses the word ἀνίστημι to say [God] *raised* him from the dead."[40] Duling

---

mans, 1982), 63.

[34]James R. Edwards, 41.

[35]van Iersel, 73.

[36]F. F. Bruce, *The Book of Acts* (Grand Rapids: Wm. B. Eerdmans, 1981), 275-76.

[37]Everett F. Harrison, *Acts: The Expanding Church* (Chicago: Moody Press, 1975), 212-13.

[38]I. Howard Marshall, "The Divine Sonship of Jesus," 87-103; Brendon Byrne, 63.

[39]Marshall, "The Divine Sonship of Jesus," 96.

[40]Eduard Schweizer, "The Concept of the Davidic 'Son of God' in Acts and Its Old Testament Background," in *Studies in Luke-Acts* (Nashville, TN: Abingdon

sees the use of ἀνίστημι as not only a reference to the resurrection, but as the New Testament counterpart of the Old Testament act of enthronement.[41] Based on his findings in intertestamental *pesher* literature, Goldsmith says, "The complex of OT citations in Acts 13:33-37 is . . . carefully conceived on linguistic and theological grounds to show the Jews *how* God fulfilled his promise to David in 2 Sam 7--namely, by raising Jesus from the dead."[42]

The argument seems to swing to the side asserting that the affirmation of Jesus' Sonship by the resurrection is to be seen as a veiled prophecy in the Old Testament. Otto Betz says, "The Christological creed [of the resurrection] remains in the framework of the Old Testament tradition . . . [and] Easter could therefore be understood in the light of the prophecy of Nathan."[43]

In the Old Testament tradition, Jesus also functioned as prophet and priest like the Messiah-son.[44] It has already been seen that God's words, "listen to him" at the transfiguration recall the promise concerning the coming prophet in Deut. 18:15. The connection with Moses extends further. Commenting on the rabbinic *Qoheleth Rabba* 1,8, James Martyn notes that the Messiah, like Moses, was expected to ride upon a donkey, to cause manna to descend and to cause waters to gush forth.[45] The priestly function of Christ is most clearly seen in his death. After surveying several New Testament passages that speak of Christ's "sacrifice" (including Rom. 3:21-26, "ἱλαστήριον . . . in his blood"), Leopold Sabourin says,

> If Christ freely gave his life in sacrifice for the redemption of mankind it is as a priest that he did it. It should be legitimately concluded that even if Christ is not explicitly called priest outside [the book of] Hebrews it is implied that he is in texts that present his death as a sacrifice.[46]

Press, 1966), 186.

[41]Dennis Duling, "The Promises to David and Their Entrance into Christianity--Nailing Down a Likely Hypothesis," *New Testament Studies* 20 (1973):71.

[42]Dale Goldsmith, "Acts 13:33-37: A *Pesher* on 2 Sam. 7," *Journal of Biblical Literature* 87 (1968):324.

[43]Otto Betz, 97.

[44]Oscar Cullmann, *The Christology of the New Testament*, trans. Shirley Guthrie and Charles Hall (Philadelphia: The Westminster Press, 1963), 113-14 points out that the Messiah, the "Anointed One" was not the only one anointed in the Old Testament. Priests were anointed when ordained (Exod. 28.41) and some prophets were anointed into office (e.g. Elisha, 1 Kings 19:16).

[45]James Louis Martyn, *History and Theology in the Fourth Gospel* (New York: Harper & Row, 1968), 99-100.

[46]Leopold Sabourin, *Priesthood: A Comparative Study*, 215.

Perhaps the single most difficult facet of Jesus' ministry to be seen as part of the Old Testament concept of Son of God is that of miracle-worker. Robert Fortna says, "There is surprisingly little direct evidence that the Jewish Messiah was expected to be a worker of miracles."[47]

But the working of miracles was considered by Jesus to mark his work as Messiahship. When imprisoned, John the Baptist sent to ask if Jesus was indeed the "Coming One." Jesus answered with a declaration of his miracles (Matt. 11:1-6 par.)[48] Jesus' preaching of the "gospel of the kingdom" is tied directly to his working of miracles (Matt. 9:35 par.). When Jesus sent out his disciples to "proclaim the kingdom," he gave them power to perform miracles (Lk. 9:1-6 par.). Thus Jesus' Messiahship, the kingdom, and the working of miracles seem to be inexorably linked.

An explanation for this, as it relates to exorcism, is offered by Howard Kee. He says,

> The clue to the significance of the title Son of God in the exorcism narratives is offered in Mark 2:23-27. The images are mixed: a kingdom is divided, a dynasty is ruined by internal conflict . . . As the demons' words disclose, Jesus is the agent of God empowered to bring about their defeat and to wrest control of the world from the hand of Satan and subject it to the rule of God. This is not traditional messianic language, according to strict Jewish traditions, but it is Mark's way of understanding the one ordained to be God's vice-gerent.[49]

At this point, Jeremias' insight into the concept of "kingdom" is helpful,

> One thing is certain: the word *malkuta* did not have for the oriental the significance that the word "kingdom" does for the westerner. Only in quite isolated instances in the Old Testament does *malkut* denote a realm in the spatial sense, a territory;

---

[47]Robert Fortna, *The Gospel of Signs* (Cambridge: Cambridge University Press, 1970), 230.

[48]Jesus' words in v. 6, "and blessed is he who refrains from stumbling over me," is probably a reference to the doubt of John and others who may not have seen Jesus' ministry as perfectly fulfilling that of the anticipated Messiah. The greatest stumbling block, that of the cross, was yet to come.

[49]Kee, *Community of the New Age* (Philadelphia: The Westminster Press, 1977), 123-24.

almost always it stands for the government, the authority, the power of the king. . . . *malkut* is always in process of being achieved. Thus the reign of God is neither a spatial nor a static concept; it is a *dynamic concept* [ital. his].[50]

Consequently, Jesus' Messiahship and Sonship in his first advent entailed something other than a physical throne and dominion over Israel's political enemies. As Kingsbury points out, Jesus' miracles (and exorcism in particular) show him to be the Son of God engaged in eschatological conflict with Satan and his forces.[51] We have seen that perhaps the people did not expect a purely political Messiah. Nonetheless, their expectation of political power with respect to the kingdom is evident (cf. Mk. 10:37).

William Wrede postulated that the "Messianic secret" was evident because Mark needed to insert a rationale in his Gospel for Jesus' life passing without Messianic fulfillment.[52] It seems more feasible to see the apparent "secret" of Jesus' Messiahship not in a lack of fulfillment, but in the lack of understanding by the people. As is evident from several passages, they were so ripe for the arrival of their anticipated Messiah that they wanted to make him king "by force" (e.g. Jn. 6:15). Thus Jesus exhorted most of those whom he healed to be silent about his Messiahship, including demons (cf. Mk. 1:25, 34). Realizing the mania that could spread among the people, Jesus admonished the cleansed leper to show himself to the priest "for a testimony to them" (Mk. 1:44). The word "them" is probably a reference to the Jewish leaders. These were the ones primarily responsible for recognizing the Messiah and designating him as such. Only then could the people be unified in their recognition of and submission to him.

But the common people did see Jesus in the role of Messiah. Just how they saw him as such in light of the working of miracles may lie in his function as "Son of David." In most references, this title is associated with healing and exorcism (e.g. Matt. 9:27; 12:22; 15:22; etc.).

Kingsbury shows that the title "Messiah" in the Gospels is equivalent to "Son of God" "King of Israel," and "Son of David."[53] In the Old Testament, aside from the one reference to Absalom (2 Sam. 13:1), the only person designated "son of David" was Solomon (1 Chr.

---

[50]Jeremias, *New Testament Theology*, 98.

[51]Kingsbury, 77.

[52]William Wrede, *The Messianic Secret*, trans, J. C. G. Grieg (London: James Clarke, 1971), passim, esp. 211-30.

[53]Kingsbury, 55.

29:22; 2 Chr. 1:1; Prov. 1:1; Eccles. 1:1). In each of these contexts, Solomon is not only called "son of David," but reference is also made to his being the king of Israel. In the last section we saw how the Old Testament references to God's "son" could only be applied to Solomon, definitively. Loren Fischer thinks that during the time of Jesus, at the popular level, the title "Son of David" referred to Solomon.[54] Thus, there may have been something conveyed by the "son" titles as applied to Jesus which looked back to the figure of Solomon.[55]

There is evidence, in fact, to substantiate this. Donahue says that in the Gospels, ". . . exorcism distinguishes a person as possessor of royal power in David's line."[56] Klaus Berger goes further and proposes that the Jewish tradition concerning Solomon's power over demons stands behind the understanding of the title "Son of David" in the New Testament.[57] Vermes shows that in intertestamental Judaism and that current with early Christianity, Solomon was viewed as an exorcist and that exorcisms were performed in his name.[58] In a passage from *Antiquities* Josephus says of Solomon,

> And God granted him knowledge of the art used against demons for the benefit and healing of men. He also composed incantations by which illnesses are relieved, and left behind forms of exorcisms with which those possessed by demons drive them out, never to return.[59]

When and how this tradition about Solomon began can only be topics of speculation. But Fischer claims that Solomon's fame as a great wonder-worker spread into many forms of Near Eastern literature.[60] That it was recognized during Jesus' time might be seen in Matt. 12:38-42. In response to the Pharisees' demand for a miraculous sign Jesus replies, "One greater than Solomon is here."

Vermes theorizes that the exorcism tradition associated with

---

[54]Loren Fischer, "'Can This Be the Son of David?'" in *Jesus and the Historian* ed. F. Thomas Trotter (Philadelphia: Fortress Press, 1968), 90.

[55]That the title "Son of David" had more meaning for Jews than non-Jews may be reflected by its nine occurences in Matthew, three in Mark, two in Luke's Gospel, but is not to be found in the rest of the New Testament.

[56]John R. Donahue, "Temple, Trial, and Royal Christology," 75.

[57]Klaus Berger, "Die königlichen Messiastraditionen des Neuen Testaments," *New Testament Studies* 20 (1973):3-9, 13-15.

[58]Geza Vermes, *Jesus the Jew* (New York: MacMillan Publishing Co., 1973), 62-65.

[59]Josephus, *Jewish Antiquities*, trans. H. St. Thackeray (Cambridge, MA: Harvard University Press, 1934), 8.45.

[60]Fischer, 85.

Solomon may stand behind the dialogue between Jesus and the Pharisees in Matt. 12:22-29. Here they accuse Jesus of casting out demons by the power of Beelzebul. Probably, says Vermes, this is because Jesus does not invoke any human source, such as that most commonly used: Solomon.[61] Thus in v. 27 Jesus retorts, "by whom do your sons cast them out?"

Jesus continues in this Matthean pericope to declare that exorcism demonstrates that "the kingdom of God has come" (v. 28). In correspondence with the Old Testament, then, the Son of David and his work are tied to the kingdom.

But Jesus' activity as "Son of David" is more than exorcistic, it is "therapeutic."[62] Obviously demon possession was viewed as a plague of evil in Palestine,[63] but the influence of evil from Satan was seen to go even further. As Vermes says,

> In the world of Jesus, the devil was believed to be at the basis of sickness as well as sin. The idea [existed] that demons were responsible for all moral and physical evil.[64]

Loader sees Jesus functioning as Messiah and Son of David to purge Israel of evil and the reign of Satan.[65]

The kingdom of which Jesus speaks and which he manifests encompasses more than a following of people and the changing of lives. It is a cataclysmic restructuring of the fallen created order. Jesus was seen as the "Son of David" because he was bringing about the anticipated "shalom" which even Solomon--the first king of peace and son of David--did not. As Messiah ("Son of David" and "Son of God"), he healed the sick, cast out demons, raised the dead (Jn. 11:27ff.), and calmed the storm (Matt. 14:22-33). Of this last account Otto Betz says, "Jesus' walking on the water proclaims his victory over the powers of chaos."[66] Jesus brought order out of chaos, he

---

[61]Vermes, 63-64.

[62]Dennis Duling, "The Therapeutic Son of David: An Element in Matthew's Christological Apologetic," *New Testament Studies* 24 (1977-78):409.

[63]Otto Betz *What Do We Know about Jesus?*, 70.

[64]Vermes, 61.

[65]W. R. G. Loader, "Son of David, Blindness, Possession, and Duality in Matthew," *Catholic Biblical Quarterly* 44 (1982):570-85.

[66]Otto Betz, p. 69, n. 52. Betz (Ibid.) also mentions the chaos Jesus overcame by his being with the "wild beasts" (Mk. 1:13). Hans-Günter Leder, "Sundenfaller-zählung und Versuchungsgeschichte," *Zeitschrift für die neutestamentliche Wissenschaft* 54 (1963):205-206, 211, referring to Old Testament texts such as Isa. 11:6-8 and Hos. 2:18, sees Jesus' presence in the wilderness with the wild beasts as an allusion to the eschatological age of salvation when men and beasts will dwell

brought about soundness, health, and well-being. In short, he brought peace. As we saw in the previous chapter, this was the responsibility of the king in the ancient world. In Nolan's words,

> The royal ideology of the Old Testament is certainly tributary to early oriental ideas of the king as mediator of the cosmic order, as guarantor of Maat or ṣedeq. By his righteousness (ṣᵉdaqah) he triumphs over enemies and ensures the Shalom of his people. He is . . . the son of God.[67]

Jesus' righteousness and provision of peace was that about which not even Solomon could boast.[68] And only in the person and work of the king did the ancient Near East see the possibility of security and peace for the people.[69] No wonder the Jews longed for the appearing of their Messiah. Some intertestamental literature summed up the blessings of the Messianic period with the word *shalom*.[70]

But Jesus' ministry *did* involve the changing of lives. As we saw earlier, the Messiah-son is more than a political king, he is a prophet and priest. Of Jesus' words in Matt. 12:42 ("a greater One than Solomon is here"), Schniewind says,

> Now what kings possessed and what prophets longed for is fulfilled. Here is a summons to repentance greater than the summons of the prophets, and a joyous word greater than the word of the first son of David. Here is God's Messiah who is both king and prophet.[71]

As prophet, Jesus' ministry is religious. But this does not conflict with some uses שָׁלוֹם of in the Old Testament. As Roth points out, in Joshua through 2 Kings the word שָׁלוֹם has religious as well as political overtones.[72] Von Rad says, "[When] used in its full compass,

---

together in peace.

[67]Brian Nolan, *The Royal Son of God* (Fribourg: Editions universitares, 1979), 225-26. See W. Malcolm Clark, "The Righteousness of Noah," *Vetus Testamentum* 21 (1971): 277-79 for a similar discussion.

[68]Thus Jesus says, "a greater one than Solomon is here" (Matt. 12:42 par).

[69]Henri Frankfort, *Kingship and the Gods*, 3.

[70]*Theological Dictionary of the New Testament*, s.v. "εἰρήνη," by Werner Foerster 2 (1964):409.

[71]Julius Schniewind, *Das Evangelium nach Matthäus*, reprint ed. (Göttingen: Vandenhoeck & Ruprecht, 1962), 163. See Appendix for this quote in German.

[72]Wolfgang Roth, "The Language of Peace: Shalom and Eirene," *Explor* 3 (1977):71.

shalom is a religious term."[73] Jesus uses this term to proclaim "go in peace (εἰρήνη), your faith has saved (root σώζω) you" (Mk. 5:34 par.; Lk. 7:50). The connection of םולש with salvation is apparent in much Old Testament usage. Citing several passages in the prophets including Jer. 31:6, Beasley-Murray says that, for the Jew, peace extended to one's existence in relation to God and others, for peace is an all-encompassing synonym for salvation.[74]

Peace was something for which the Jew longed. Van Rad says, "Expectation of a final state of eternal peace is an element in OT eschatology which finds constant expression in the prophets and other writings."[75] As the Jews longed for this peace, so Jesus' ministry was characterized by peace. It was prophesied of him by Isaiah ("Prince of Peace," 9:6), announced at his birth (Lk. 2:14), prophesied by Zacharias to define his ministry (Lk. 1:79), an essential part of the disciples' ministry as a reflection of his (Matt. 10:13 par.), proclaimed by the people in association with him at the Triumphal Entry (Lk. 19:38), that which was rejected by Israel when they rejected him (Lk. 19:42), and that which Jesus left for those who believe in him (Jn. 14:27; 16:33; 20:19, 21-22, 26).[76]

Thus Jesus announced the kingdom over which neither Solomon--the "king of peace"--nor any other Israelite king had reigned. Jesus showed himself to be God's anointed, God's representative, and God's Son in his conquering the forces of evil which had prevailed over the cosmos.[77] Betz says Jesus' miracles are essentially "victories over death and the devil."[78]

In summary, it appears evident from our examination of Jesus' Sonship as Messiah, that the concept definitely has Old Testament roots. As Kingsbury says, the titles "Messiah," "King of Israel," "Son of David," and "Son of God" are not only synonymous in the Gospels, but are "part and parcel of the same Old Testament and Jewish imagery."[79] The titles and the reaction of the people to Jesus' ministry demonstrate the truth of Longenecker's observation that "for the disciples it was the conviction of Jesus as Messiah . . . which

---

[73]*Theological Dictionary of the New Testament*, s.v."εἰρήνη," by Gerhard von Rad, 2(1965):403.

[74]George R. Beasley-Murray, *Jesus and the Kingdom of God* (Grand Rapids: William B. Eerdmans, 1986), 20.

[75]von Rad, "εἰρήνη," 2:405.

[76]Notice Jesus' blessing on the "peacemakers" who shall be called "sons of God" (Matt. 5:9).

[77]Jesus said Satan was the "ruler of the cosmos" (Jn. 12:31; 14:30; 16:11).

[78]Otto Betz, 69.

[79]Kingsbury, *The Christology of Mark's Gospel*, 64.

was the basic datum in their understanding of Jesus."[80] Jesus certainly fulfilled the requirements for Israel's king. He was of the house and lineage of David (Lk. 2:4). He was declared to be God's Son --which in the Old Testament tradition indicated the king--on the three occasions of his birth, baptism, and resurrection.[81]

The problem in the assertion that Jesus' ministry manifested him as Israel's Messiah is that much of what he did hardly seems appropriate for a king. But Jewish Messiahship meant more than being a political figure. The Messiah-son was both political and religious in his office.[82] This is evident from the prophetic and priestly functions of David and Solomon.

The Old Testament is therefore a testimony to Jesus as Messiah. As van Ruler says, to legitimatize Jesus as Messiah the Old Testament is necessary in order to ascertain what the Messianic works of God are.[83] Nolan outlines what those Messianic works entail,

> The Bible [i.e. Old Testament] . . . has connected wisdom and temple with the Davidic king--and creation, salvation, and the spirit with all three. In the religious moulding of Israel these five realities cluster around the significant individual, the king. At the threshold of Christianity there existed a mystical respect for the Davidic guarantor of the Temple, for the all-wise Anointed, for the spirit-filled monarch at Jerusalem whose righteousness brought Shalom, and who shared as Son and heir the cosmic sway of Yahweh--in particular by his power over the evil spirits. . . .The Gospel portrait or, rather, motion picture of Jesus, the Son of David and beloved Son of God, shepherding the Twelve tribes in the power of the Spirit, living out the Torah, and definition . . . when viewed against a faith nourished on Davidic mysticism.[84]

This heightened Davidic mysticism and expectation of the "Son of

---

[80]Richard N. Longenecker, *The Christology of Early Jewish Christianity*, 96.

[81]W. Malcolm Clark (p. 279), says these correspond to the Old Testament's "three moments" in the life of the king: the decision by God before birth (1 Chr. 22:9); the ceremonial revelation of the election (1 Sam. 16) and the installation into office (Ps. 2:7).

[82]Walter Grundmann, "Sohn Gottes. Ein Diskussionsbeitrag," *Zeitschrift für die neutestamentliche Wissenschaft* 47 (1956):113-33 shows, based on evidence from Qumran texts, that there was some speculation concerning a Messianic high priest who would be called "Son of God."

[83]Arnold A. Van Ruler, *The Christian Church and the Old Testament*, trans. Geoffrey W. Bromiley (Grand Rapids: Wm. B. Eerdmans, 1971), 70-71.

[84]Nolan, 231.

David" within Judaism is probably the rationale for not seeing the title "Son of David" in reference to Jesus outside of Palestine. As with the title "king of Israel," it had significance only for Jews.

Jesus was thus the Messiah who was bringing the longed-for peace. In so-doing he was the unique Son of God. But the leaders, whom Jesus would have had recognize his Sonship (Mk. 1:44), repeatedly rejected him. The kingdom was thus taken from them to be given to another (Matt. 21:43).

These concepts of peace, sonship, and king flow together in Isaiah's prophecy. He says the "son," the "prince of peace" is the one who will be born to sit on David's throne, whose kingdom of peace will be without end, and who will be called "the Mighty God" (Isa. 9:6-7).

This last title points to a broader meaning for the concept of Jesus' Sonship than does the title "Messiah." As Reginald Fuller states, "Jesus is not the Son because he is the Messiah . . . The Sonhood is the basis of his Messiahship, not the Messiahship the basis of his Sonhood."[85] Vincent Taylor adds,

> The title [Son of God] reveals the Messianic idea in eclipse. . . . Sometimes the meaning is Messianic, but . . . it is Messianic with a plus. . . . And when St. Paul says that "in the fullness of time God sent forth his Son" (Gal. 4:4), we have passed far beyond the idea of a divinely commissioned national deliverer to the thought of One who comes to our world from the depths of the being of God.[86]

That broader meaning which eclipses Jewish Messianism is the subject of the next section. Let us proceed to examine Jesus' Sonship as an expression of his filial relationship with God.

Jesus the Son of God: the unique filial relationship with God

The most frequently-used word in Jesus' reference to God is that of "Father." Jeremias observes that in all his personal conversations

---

[85]Reginald H. Fuller, *The Mission and Achievement of Jesus* (London: SCM Press, Ltd., 1954), 84.

[86]Vincent Taylor, *The Names of Jesus* (New York: St. Martin's Press, 1953), 70.

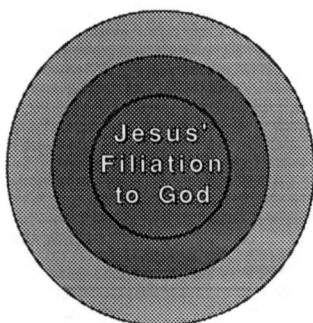

with God, i.e. in prayer, Jesus addresses him as "Father."[87] While the Old Testament does use this image to refer to God, it does so only fourteen times. The Judaism of the Intertestamental period continues this reluctance. But in contrast to this, Jesus refers to God as his Father no less than 125 times in the four Gospels.[88]

This terminology, says Marshall, is based on Jesus' consciousness of a unique filial relationship to God rather than on his Messiahship. He explains, "The fundamental point in Jesus' self-understanding was his filial relationship to God and that it was from this basic conviction that he undertook the tasks variously assigned to the Messiah . . . rather than that the basic datum was consciousness of being the Messiah."[89] In this vein William Lane says of the baptism narrative,

> In this context "Son" is not a messianic title, but is to be understood in the highest sense, transcending messiahship. It signifies the unique relationship Jesus sustains to the Father, which exists apart from any thought of official function in history: Jesus is God's unique Son. . . . Jesus did not *become* the Son of God, at the baptism or at the transfiguration; he *is* the Son of God.[90]

Edwards' explanation of the relationship of Messiah to Son of God is well-stated,

> If "Son of God" and "Christ" were [exactly] synonymous one would expect to find "Christ" in the text of the baptism. . . . "My Son," however, is accompanied by ἀγαπητός, an adjective describing a filial relationship, not by χριστός. Jesus is God's anointed, the Messiah, only because he first is the son who is cherished by the Father and pleasing to him. The status of Sonship, therefore,

---

[87]Jeremias, *New Testament Theology*, 1:62.

[88]*The International Standard Bible Encyclopedia*, Rev. ed., s.v. "ABBA," by David E. Aune, 1:3.

[89]Marshall, "The Divine Sonship of Jesus," *Interpretation* 21 (1967):93.

[90]William L. Lane, *The Gospel of Mark* (Grand Rapids: Wm. B. Eerdmans, 1974), 57-58.

precedes the function of Messiahship.[91]

This filial relationship actually corresponds well with the Old Testament concept of sonship. As we saw, obedience was required of the "son," Israel, in the Old Testament. Jeremias points out that this is borne out in Intertestamental literature, also. The "sons" of God are those who show obedience to God.[92]

Jesus' ministry is characterized by his obedience to the Father. Nolan says,

> The close association of sonship and obedience . . . is apparent in the Gospels . . . But it is Matthew who, in his rather stark manner, points up the sonlike obedience of Jesus. His simplest technique is his use of "the will of the Father" e.g. 7:21; 12:50; 18:12; 21:31; 26:42. The first evangelist also presents Jesus as the one who perfected and fulfilled the will of the Father. . . . Baptism of the Son to fulfill all righteousness, the testing of the Son who knew the word of God, submission to the Father in . . . Gethsemane, the obedience of the derided Son on the cross--all are instances of Jesus being a model of docile sonship.[93]

Lamar Williamson says of Matt. 4:1-11,

> The unit is related to the context in Matthew in two important ways. First, it confirms the divine attestation of Jesus as Son of God through the voice from heaven at his baptism (3:17). . . . Second, the temptation is closely related to the crucifixion. . . . At the beginning of his ministry, Jesus is tempted to win public acclaim by a dramatic miracle; at the end he is taunted by the challenge to demonstrate his divine sonship by saving his life. . . . By his costly obedience, Jesus shows that he is the Son of God.[94]

This absolute fidelity demonstrated in his obedience shows Jesus' sonship to parallel that of Israel's in the Old Testament. Intertestamental literature emphasized the requirement of obedience for Israel as God's "son." Byrne says that in this literature, "The 'sonship of God' theme occurs with considerable frequency in eschatological

---

[91]J. R. Edwards, "The Son of God: Its Antecedents in Judaism and Hellenism and Its Use in the Earliest Gospel," 107.

[92]Jeremias, *The Prayers of Jesus*, 18-19.

[93]Nolan, 218-19.

[94]Lamar Williamson, "Matthew 4:1-11," *Interpretation* 38 (1984):51.

contexts, suggesting that it was an epithet felt to be particularly applicable to the ideal Israel."[95] According to Strack-Billerbeck, the reference to Israel as God's "son" was a common epithet of the rabbis.[96] Reginald Fuller articulates how Jesus fits into this framework of Israel's sonship,

> Now to the Hebrew mind the father-son relationship . . . connoted favour and care on the part of the father, and the response of filial love, authority on the one side, and obedience on the other. In particular, by obedient submission to the father's will, the son becomes a perfect reproduction of his father at every point. The Father-Son relationship in which Jesus knew himself to stand is a relationship involving choice and response, authority and obedience. The basic pattern for this relationship is to be found in the sonship of Israel in the Old Testament.[97]

Examples of Jesus as the ideal and faithful "son" paralleling Israel in the Old Testament include the instances of the voice from heaven. Here Jesus is called the beloved ($\dot{a}\gamma a\pi\eta\tau\delta s$) Son (Matt. 3:17 par.; 17:5 par.; 2 Pet. 1:17). Kee points out that there are three Old Testament texts which could lie behind these passages: Gen. 22:2 (Abraham's son Isaac), Isa. 42:1 (the chosen servant of Yahweh) and Exod. 4:22 (Israel is called God's "firstborn son"). Bretscher holds that Exod 4:22 is the best possibility when the LXX and 2 Peter are seen in comparison:

Exod. 4:22 - $\dot{o}$ $\upsilon\iota\delta s$ $\mu o\upsilon$ $\dot{o}$ $\pi\rho\omega\tau\delta\tau o\kappa o s$ $\mu o\upsilon$ '$I\sigma\rho a\dot{\eta}\lambda$ ($\dot{\epsilon}\sigma\tau\iota\nu$)

2 Pet. 1:17 - $\dot{o}$ $\upsilon\iota\delta s$ $\mu o\upsilon$ $\dot{o}$ $\dot{a}\gamma a\pi\eta\tau\delta s$ $\mu o\upsilon$ $o\dot{\upsilon}\tau o s$ $\dot{\epsilon}\sigma\tau\iota\nu$

Bretscher says that, "Whether Jesus as the Son of God is called $\dot{a}\gamma a\pi\eta\tau\delta s$ or $\mu o\nu o\gamma\epsilon\nu\dot{\eta}s$ or $\dot{\epsilon}\kappa\lambda\dot{\epsilon}\kappa\tau o s$, the root term which seems to stand behind all these is $\pi\rho\omega\tau\delta\tau o\kappa o s$, answering to בְּכוֹרִי of Exod. 4:22."[98] Certainly Matthew is pointing to Jesus' role as the "ideal Israel" when he says Jesus fulfills Hosea's prophecy "out of Egypt I have called My Son" (2:15).

---

[95]Byrne, 62-63.

[96]Hermann L. Strack und Paul Billerbeck, *Kommentar zum Neuen Testament aus Talmud und Midrash*, Erster Band, Das Evangelium nach Matthäus (München: C. H. Beck'sche Verlagsbuchhandlung, 1961), 219-20.

[97]Reginald H. Fuller, *The Mission and Achievement of Jesus*, 85.

[98]Paul G. Bretscher, "Exodus 4:22-23 and the Voice from Heaven," *Journal of Biblical Literature* 87 (1968):310.

Jesus clearly demonstrated absolute fidelity of obedience in his prevailing over Satan in the Temptation.[99] Besides the cross, this may have been his greatest act of obedience. But it should be noted that with each temptation from Satan, Jesus responds with a reference to a passage in Deuteronomy. That is, Jesus uses Deuteronomy exclusively to thwart Satan's temptations. Why Deuteronomy? Thompson explains,

> The parallelism with Deuteronomy at this point helps us to understand in what light the Evangelists probably interpreted the whole episode. Deut. 8:2 gives a theological interpretation of the wilderness wanderings: they had the purpose of testing and proving Israel to see whether the people of God would be loyal to their Redeemer.[100]

But Deuteronomy is also the book with more references to Israel's sonship than any other in the Old Testament. Thus Thompson continues,

> Jesus is declared to be God's Son, just as Israel's status in Deut. 8:5 is likened to that of a son. Israel is commissioned and tested: the same experience of Jesus . . . the beginning of the ministry of Jesus follows the same pattern as the call of Israel.[101]

The main theme of the Temptation narrative, therefore, "seems to be the obedience of Jesus seen in contrast with the disobedience and rebellion of Israel of the wilderness days."[102] Reginald Fuller sees Jesus' Sonship to be "what it was intended to mean for Israel, the unquestioning response to the event of God's choice by unswerving obedience to his will."[103] Cullmann also sees obedience as the essence of Sonship for Jesus. He states,

> The most important passages of the Synoptic Gospels in which Jesus appears as the Son of God show him precisely . . . as one radically and uniquely distinguished from all other men . . . to

---

99Gunther Bornkamm, Gerhard Barth, and Heinz Joachim Held, *Tradition and Interpretation in Matthew*, trans. Percy Scott (London: SCM Press, 1963), 37.

100G. H. P. Thompson, "Called--Proved--Obedient: A Study in the Baptism and Temptation Narrative of Matthew and Luke," *Journal of Theological Studies* 11 (1960):1.

101Ibid., 2.

102Ibid., 7.

103Fuller, *The Mission and Achievement of Jesus*, 85.

fulfill his task in complete unity with the Father. This distinction . . . means the absolute obedience of a son in the execution of a divine commission.[104]

This obedience was not just a pattern of life for Jesus. It led him to the cross. Because of this, Moule sees Jesus as "uniquely identified with God precisely by his unique degree of submission to the will of God."[105] Bauckham says,

> This obedience, of course, is not the obedience of the slave but the obedience of the Son, who in love willingly identifies himself with the Father's purpose. . . . [thus] The credibility of his claim to unique Sonship cannot be separated from his path to the cross.[106]

Kingsbury says the words of the centurion at the cross manifest his observing one "who is utterly obedient to and places his total trust in God."[107] Cullmann sees the concepts of Jesus' Sonship and obedience unto death stemming from the Old Testament,

> . . . as the "Son of God" from the beginning, [Jesus] has been obedient to the Father's plan of salvation. Thus we find that . . . the Son of God carries out the divine plan of salvation in his life, but above all in his death. God did not "spare" his own Son, writes Paul in Rom. 8:32, recalling the story of Abraham's sacrifice of Isaac . . .[108]

Jesus' Sonship is seen most clearly, however, in his intimate relationship to God. This relationship is demonstrated in his unique knowledge of the Father (e.g. Matt. 11:27), which McDermott shows has background in "Qumran discoveries which testified clearly to Jewish conceptions of 'knowledge' as personal, intimate, and often mediated."[109] Marshall says of Jesus' words in Matt. 11:27 ("no one knows the Son except the Father, no one knows the Father except the Son") that, "Its Semitic character shows that it is not of Hellenistic

---

[104]Oscar Cullmann, *Christology of the New Testament*, 276.

[105]C. F. D. Moule, "The New Testament and the Doctrine of the Trinity," *Expository Times* 88(1976):17.

[106]Richard Bauckham, "The Sonship of the Historical Jesus in Christology," *Scottish Journal Theology* 31(1978): 257.

[107]Kingsbury, *The Christology of Mark's Gospel*, 131.

[108]Cullmann, 292-93.

[109]McDermott, "Jesus and the Son of God Title," *Gregorianum* 62 (1981):288.

origin; in particular the formulation of the mutual relationship of Father and Son can be paralleled from Semitic sources as a type of expression necessary in language which (unlike Greek) possess no reciprocal pronoun."[110]

The uniqueness of Jesus' Sonship is reflected in the adjectives associated with "Son." He is the "beloved" ($\dot{a}\gamma a\pi\eta\tau\acute{o}\varsigma$) Son. Marshall says this shows Jesus' Sonship to go "beyond a purely functional or messianic use of the title [to indicate] the unique relationship of Jesus to his Father."[111] But the most significant adjective used in this regard is $\mu o\nu o\gamma\epsilon\nu\acute{\eta}\varsigma$. Dale Moody shows that this word cannot mean "begotten" for it bears no effective relationship to $\gamma\epsilon\nu\nu\acute{a}\omega$.[112] "Only-begotten" is $\mu o\nu o\gamma\acute{\epsilon}\nu\nu\eta\tau o\varsigma$, a term used in the first century.[113] Rather, $\mu o\nu o\gamma\epsilon\nu\acute{\eta}\varsigma$ stems from $\mu\acute{o}\nu o\varsigma$ (one) and $\gamma\acute{\epsilon}\nu o\varsigma$ (kind) to indicate "only," "one of a kind," or "unique."[114] Jesus is thus the *unique* Son of God.

It is in Jesus' reference to and communication with God that we see his unique Sonship expressed most evidently. As van Iersel points out, Jesus never included himself in the address "our Father." Rather, he was careful to distinguish between "my Father" and "your Father."[115] The most exhaustive study on this issue was done by Jeremias.[116] He says, "In the literature of Palestinian Judaism no evidence has yet been found of 'my Father' being used by an individual as an address to God."[117] This demonstrates Jesus' unique and incommunicable relationship to God.

But when Jesus employs the term "*Abba*" he best illuminates this filial relationship. This term, ". . . was a children's word, used in everyday talk, an expression of courtesy. It would have seemed disrespectful, indeed unthinkable, to the sensibilities of Jesus' contemporaries to address God with this familiar word."[118] The term meant "Daddy" and was used only by a child to address his own father.[119] But the term did not necessarily convey a presence of naivety, for it

---

110Marshall, "The Divine Sonship of Jesus," 91.

111Idem, "Son of God or Servant of Yahweh?--A Reconsideration of Mark 1:11," *New Testament Studies* 15 (1968-69): 336.

112Dale Moody, "God's Only Son: The Translation of John 3:16 in the Revised Standard Version," *Journal of Biblical Literature* 72 (1953):213.

113*The Vocabulary of the Greek Testament*, by James Hope Moulton and George Milligan, s.v. "$\mu o\nu o\gamma\epsilon\nu\acute{\eta}\varsigma$," 416-17.

114Moody, 213.

115van Iersel, *Der Sohn in den Synoptischen Jesusworten*, 93-104.

116Richard Bauckham (245) says, "It is unlikely that subsequent research will be able to do more than [merely] modify his conclusions."

117Jeremias, *New Testament Theology*, 64.

118Ibid., 67.

119Idem, *The Prayers of Jesus*, 58-59.

was occasionally used by an adult offspring to address the father.[120] Because the use of this term was viewed as radical and would have been offensive to contemporary Judaism, Jesus reserves it exclusively for personal prayer or private instruction.[121]

In summary, we see that Jesus possessed an exclusive and incommunicable Sonship to God.[122] It was a Sonship which cannot be viewed as adoptionistic. As one writer says, had the Gospel writers held to adoptionism, they would have stated so expressly in order to counteract any alternative view in the Early Church. That they omitted any mention of adoptionism must indicate they did not espouse it, themselves.[123]

Jesus' filial relationship with God points to the essence of his Sonship. Neill shows that in the Jewish community of Jesus' day, the intense tradition of family loyalty and family continuity meant that sonship would have included the stages of obedience to, understanding of and cooperation with the parent.[124]

Jesus' relationship to the Father corresponds with that typified by Israel in the pages of the Pentateuch. Just as "in first century Judaism the ideas of Israel as God's son and the anointed king as God's son existed side by side," so it is for the person of Jesus.[125] His Sonship as the Messiah and as an expression of his relationship with God are inexorably bound together. Schweizer says, "Thus the question of the relation between the unique divine sonship of the coming Davidic king and that of the whole people of Israel, still open in post-biblical Judaism (cf. Ps. Sol. 17), is answered in the New Testament by the person of Jesus Christ."[126]

But Jesus is the Messiah because he is the Son, not vice-versa. Just as the king was first of all an Israelite and part of the community called God's "son," so Jesus is first the Son by his filial relationship with God. Of this filiation Howton says it is "a representation and self-communication on the part of God . . . which is designed to lead to the self-revelation of God."[127]

---

[120]Ibid., 60.

[121]McDermott, 279.

[122]van Iersel, 183.

[123]Philip George Davis, "'Truly this Man Was the Son of God': The Christological Focus of the Markan Redaction," 146.

[124]Steven Neill, *The Supremacy of Jesus* (Downers Grove, IL: InterVarsity Press, 1984), 101-17.

[125]Richard Longenecker, *The Christology of Early Jewish Christianity*, 97.

[126]Eduard Schweizer, "The Concept of the Davidic 'Son of God' in Acts and Its Old Testament Background," in *Studies in Luke-Acts* (Nashville, TN: Abingdon Press, 1966), 191.

[127]Dom John Howton, "'Son of God' in the Fourth Gospel," *New Testament*

Moule says that one of the major "pointers" in the New Testament which implies Jesus' equality with God is the use of the Father-Son language. Although it may be seen as parabolic in some cases, he says, "When 'the Father' and 'the Son' seem to be taken beyond the merely parabolic, and used almost as independent technical terms, we are . . . witnessing a tacit recognition of the character of the Deity as involving reciprocity and dialogue."[128]

As the beloved Son, Jesus is sent by God to "mediate the gracious presence of his Father to others."[129] This sending formula is "in accordance with the Semitic conception of representation in which the son . . . is . . . the plenipotentary [of the father]."[130] As Kim points out, rabbinic Judaism saw "the one sent by a man is as the man himself."[131] Jesus' Sonship designates him as the One sent by the Father to do his work and to be his unique representative. The next section examines the ramifications of Jesus' Sonship as a designation of sharing God's nature.

Jesus the Son of God: the unique identification with God

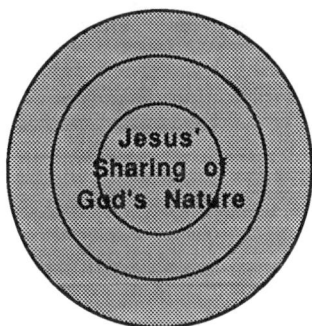

The preceding two sections examined the Christological title Son of God and found it to appear first as "functional." That is, Jesus was seen by his contemporaries as the Son of God primarily because he demonstrated the works of the anticipated Messiah. He also showed his Sonship by his perfect obedience, fulfilling God's expectation for his son Israel. The previous section moved, however, from the aspect of function to that of relationship. Jesus was called the Son because of his unique affiliation with God. These concepts of sonship are consistent with those seen in the Old Testament. The "sons" of God--Israel and the Messiah--were designated as such both because of their special covenant relationship with their Father and because of their function in office and obedience.

Studies 10 (1963-64):236.

128C. F. D. Moule, "The New Testament and the Doctrine of the Trinity," 17.

129Bauckham, 250.

130Seyoon Kim, *The Origin of Paul's Gospel*, 119.

131 Ibid.

The present section emphasizes the fuller relational aspect of Jesus' Sonship. Indeed, the designation "Son of God" as applied to Jesus implies more than a mere functional role, it expresses the unique relationship between Jesus and God.[132] This relationship is that which Edwards says "contains implications of shared status and nature."[133] Thus Jesus' Sonship is far more than functional, it is primarily a declaration of who Jesus is.[134]

The difficulty at this point is that in the Old Testament, the king was but a man. In the New Testament, Jesus is presented as a divine figure. Thus, like many, van Ruler says that the deity of Jesus cannot be derived from the Old Testament.[135] This assumption led Bultmann to postulate that it was not until the gospel reached the Hellenistic church that "Son of God" was seen to be a designation of Jesus' deity, for in Palestine it was simply a royal title.[136]

The question Nolan poses is of key importance, here. He asks, "What does it mean to be a 'son' for the New Testament audience?"[137] In the section on the various concepts of sonship in the Old Testament the metaphorical uses were seen to expressed three levels of relationship: "general association," "similarity to," and "identity with." In the Intertestamental period, however, the sonship terminology came to be employed in the most narrow sense to describe the nature of an individual.[138] Qumran texts speak, for example, of "sons of light" (1 QS 1:9; 2:16), "sons of righteousness" (1 QS 3:20, 22), and "sons of darkness" (1 QM 1:1, 7, 10, 16; 3:6, 9; 13:16).

This is the metaphorical usage of the term "son" which the New Testament employs. The essence of one's nature is represented by titles such as "son of peace" (Lk. 10:6), "sons of light" (Lk. 16:8; Jn. 12:36; 1 Thes. 5:5), "sons of this age" (Lk. 16:8; 20:34), "sons of the wicked one" (Matt. 13:38), "sons of the devil" (Acts 13:10; cf. Jn. 8:44), "sons of disobedience" (Eph. 2:2; 5:6), and "sons of men" (Mk. 3:38; Eph. 3:5). These uses confirm that "son" was employed in the lan-

---

132Jacob Kremer, "'Sohn Gottes.' Zur Klärung des biblischen Hoheitstitels Jesu," *Bibel und Liturgie* 46 (1973): 11.

133Edwards, 83.

134Ibid., 107.

135van Ruler, 46-47. But Johann J. Stamm ("Jesus Christ and the Old Testament," in *Essays on Old Testament Hermeneutics*, trans. Ludwig R. Dewitz, ed. James Luther Mays, (Richmond, VA: John Knox Press, 1964), 208) offers the insight that the Old Testament does give a background to the deity of Christ since the Messiah's authoritative position and designation "son" demonstrate a unique relationship to God.

136Bultmann, *Theology of the New Testament*, 1:50.

137Nolan, 216.

138Lohse, "υἱός," 8:358.

guage of the day to indicate the essential nature of the referent. The title "Son of God," therefore, could have carried more significance than merely a Messianic designation (and may be part of the reason for the apparent reticence of Intertestamental writers to employ it).

In keeping with the methodology of this chapter, this section will establish whether there is evidence from the Old Testament to substantiate New Testament claims to Jesus' deity. Such evidence may be seen when realizing that in the Old Testament, God did mighty works among his people saying, "I performed my signs . . . that you might know that I am Yahweh" (Exod. 10:2; Num. 14:11; Deut. 7:19; 29:2-3; Jer. 32:20-21). Jesus also did great miracles. In them he not only did the works of the Father (Jn. 5:19-20; 8:26-29) and as the Father's representative (Jn. 5:36), but his claim in doing them parallels the work of Yahweh in the Old Testament.[139] As Fennema says, what pious Old Testament prophet would have said "the works which *I* do" (Jn. 5:36).[140] These works bear witness of who Jesus is.[141]

Although the king in the Old Testament was only a man, the expectation of the promised Messiah necessitated a more lofty individual. Goppelt notes that in Psalm 110, "The Messiah, there, must not simply rank relatively higher than David, he must be fundamentally higher."[142] Fitzmyer points out that the term "LORD" (Yahweh) is translated κύριος in the Septuagint.[143] This is the same term used in the New Testament to designate Jesus. As Kaiser points out,[144] this is evidenced most plainly in the comparison of Zechariah 14:5 and 1 Thess. 3:13. The latter says, "at the coming of our *Lord* Jesus *with all his saints*" while the former says, "the *Lord* my God shall come and *all the saints with him.*"

---

[139]H. van der Loos, *The Miracles of Jesus* (Leiden: E. J. Brill, 1965), 701.

[140]David A. Fennema, "Jesus and God according to John: An Analysis of the Fourth Gospel's Father/Son Christology" (Ph.D. dissertation, Duke University, 1979), 140.

[141]Some have argued that Jesus never claimed to be the Son of God (but cf. Jn. 10:36) or God, and thus (even if it were true) was not conscious of such. Graham Brown ("Identity Statements and the Incarnation," *Heythrop Journal* 22 (1981):261-77) offers an apt argument to this. He says the New Testament does offer first person statements of Jesus' identity as God based on other criteria than the verbal assertion "I am God," which itself cannot be accepted as a statement of identity any more than "I am virtuous" or "I am humble." That is, God has always *demonstrated* who he is by his works.

[142]Goppelt, *Typos*, 83.

[143]Joseph Fitzmyer, *A Christological Catechism* (New York: Paulist Press, 1981), 91.

[144]Christopher B. Kaiser, *The Doctrine of God* (Westchester, IL: Crossway Books, 1982), 33

This correspondence of references both to Jesus and to the Yahweh of the Old Testament is also seen in the use of "I am," the basis of Yahweh's name in Hebrew (cf. Exod 3:14-15).[145] Ronald Youngblood says, "The transition of the Old Testament 'I AM' of Yahweh to the New Testament 'I am' of Jesus Christ is not far to seek."[146] Goppelt shows this to be most evident in the dialogue between Jesus and the high priest (Mk. 14:61-62).[147] When the priest asks if he is "the Christ, the Son of the Blessed," Jesus' response is "I am" ($\dot{\epsilon}\gamma\dot{\omega}$ $\epsilon\dot{\iota}\mu\dot{\iota}$). Thus the "Son" is equated with Yahweh in the person of Jesus Christ.

There are implications within the Old Testament for the "son" being equal to Yahweh. Proverbs 30:4 asks a series of rhetorical questions with obvious reference to Yahweh: "Who has ascended into heaven and descended? Who has gathered the wind in his fists? Who has wrapped the waters in his garment? Who has established all the ends of the earth?" The next question asks, "What is his name or his *son's* name?" J. Barton Payne sees consistency in reading Isa. 7:14 and the next four chapters as a unit.[148] The Messiah is *Immanu-El*, the "son" who will be the "mighty God" and "Father of Eternity" (9:6). There is thus a distinction to be made in the terminology of the passage. A "child" is born, but a "son" is *given*.[149] This Son has no beginning.

One more example is offered in this brief survey. There were only two men in the Old Testament who were said to have stood before the very presence of Yahweh "on the mountain" (Sinai): Moses (Exod. 33:18-23; 34:6-7) and Elijah (1 Kings 19:9-13). These two men conversed with Yahweh, himself. These are also the two men who stood before Jesus and conversed with him at his transfiguration on a "high mountain" (Matt. 17:1-8 par). The implication is unquestionable: the Yahweh of the Old Testament is the "beloved Son" of the New (Matt. 17:5 par).

Implications for deity in Jesus' Sonship are certainly seen in his works and in his claims for himself. Jesus repeatedly says he does the work of the Father (Jn. 5:17; 10:32, etc.). Lindars says the Father's work and Jesus' work are thus parallel.[150] But Fennema

---

[145]Ronald Youngblood, "A New Occurence of the Divine Name 'I Am,'" *Journal of the Evangelical Theological Society* 15:3 (1972):144.

[146]Ibid., 149.

[147]Goppelt, *Typos*, 89-90.

[148]J. Barton Payne, *The Theology of the Older Testament* (Grand Rapids: Zondervan Publishing House, 1962), 263.

[149]I am indebted to Dr. Allen P. Ross for pointing out this distinction.

[150]Barnabas Lindars, *The Gospel of John* (London: Marshall, Morgan & Scott Publishers, Ltd., 1972), 219.

says they are identical.[151] Of Jn. 5:17 Barrett says,

> The Jews are not slow to see the implications of Jesus'
> argument. . . . This assumption of a uniform activity common to
> Jesus and God could only mean that Jesus was equal to God.[152]

One aspect of Jesus' work was to exorcise demons. These beings repeatedly recognized him to be the Son of God (e.g. Mk. 1:24; 5:7, etc.). Edwards points out that this recognition (except for the voice of God at the baptism) represents the first confession of Jesus as God's Son. This is so, says Edwards, because demons are superhuman beings who share the spiritual world with God.[153] It should be noted that these demons do not merely fear and confess the God whom he serves, they confess and fear Jesus, himself.

It must not be overlooked, however, that the major work of Jesus, the Son of God, is the cross. Hengel says,

> It is remarkable that at the very point where the divine sonship
> and pre-existence of the exalted Christ are stressed . . . the
> shame of his passion also stands in the center. This is true for
> Paul, for the author of Hebrews and--in a somewhat different
> form--for the Second (Mk. 15:39) and Fourth (Jn. 19:5)
> Evangelists. The "doxa" of the Son of God cannot be separated
> from the shame of his cross.[154]

In summary, the Old Testament, Jesus' works, and his claims for himself all testify that his Sonship meant that he was to be identified with God. Vermes remarks that none of the Synoptics attempts to bridge the gulf between God and the "Son of God," because such would have been inconceivable to first-century Palestinian Jews.[155] This may be true, but Jesus' oneness with God in his works and his reciprocity in their relationship certainly presented a figure unlike any Old Testament character. In contrast with Vermes' view, Fennema explains John's description of Jesus,

> The paradoxical relationship of Father to Son represents John's
> attempt to acknowledge Jesus as God within a Jewish frame of
> reference. In brief he wishes to affirm Jesus' deity without ap-

---

151Fennema, 142.
152C. K. Barrett, *The Gospel according to St. John* (London: SPCK, 1955), 213-14.
153Edwards, 117.
154Hengel, *The Son of God*, 88.
155Vermes, 212.

pearing either to limit God's sovereignty or lapse into ditheism. For, a strict equation of Jesus to Yahweh would bind the latter to earthly existence for a generation; but an unqualified distinction between God-the-Father and God-the-Son would require belief in two Gods. John's solution is to expand the existing concept of "God" to include the Son as well as the Father. That is to say, he pictures Jesus as perfectly representing (and therefore being) the one true God, yet remaining distinct from (God) the ever-transcendent Father who sent him.[156]

Vincent Taylor offers insights into the difficulty inherent in the title, "Son of God,"

> When we attempt to say just how much is to be read into this terminology we are baffled; but the reason is undoubted. The situation is not one in which a clearly defined label, with a meaning known to all, is being used in its application to the man Jesus. The reverse is true. A man, revered, loved, and worshiped is described by a terminology which bends and cracks under the strain, because it is being used to describe a unique person, and therefore to serve an end for which, humanly speaking, it was not intended from the standpoint of its history. Divinity is felt before it is named, and when it is named the words are inadequate.[157]

This inadequacy is seen in the metaphor "son." Jesus is called such, though he had no beginning of existence as does a human son. But the metaphor breaks down further when it is realized that neither does God the Father have a beginning as does every other father.

Summary

The purpose in the examination of the Christological title "Son of God" has not been to present an exhaustive study of the title. Rather, this chapter has sought to establish whether there are any clear ties between the concepts of sonship to God in the Old Testament and Jesus' Sonship in the New. At each level of Jesus' Sonship--that of Messiah, filial relationship, and sharing of God's nature--the New Testament sees the Old Testament as the necessary background. This is because, in large part, the New Testament authors were

---

[156]Fennema, 296.

[157]Vincent Taylor, *The Names of Jesus* (London: Macmillan & Company, Ltd., 1952), 70.

Jews. Hengel says,

> The Jewish Christians were always the spiritual driving force
> which determined the content of the theology. In fact they put
> their stamp on the whole of the first century church.
> Unfortunately the history of religions school paid too little
> attention to this decisive point. The men who carried on the
> spiritual controversy with Judaism most sharply during the
> first century A.D. come from Judaism.[158]

The Son of God title, as Kingsbury notes, is the one title that
extends to *every* phase of Jesus' life and ministry: conception, birth,
infancy, baptism, temptation, public ministry (including miracles),
death, resurrection and exaltation. It is "the most fundamental
Christological category."[159]

Yet it appears that Jesus' function as Messiah was that most
readily recognized as prompting the title "Son of God" from his peers.
The use of this and other equivalent titles ("Son of David" and "King of
Israel") are used interchangeably with the designation "Christ"
during his ministry in Palestine. Cullmann shows that the Synoptic
Gospels record recognition of Jesus as Son of God only in exceptional
cases like Peter's confession which came from God (Matt. 16:17), the
reference by Satan (Matt. 4:3, 6), by demons (Mk. 3:11; 5:7) and by
God's voice at the baptism and transfiguration.[160] Dunn points out
that the crowd of John's Gospel appears to question the designation
"Christ" rather than confess Jesus as such (e.g. 7:26-31). This
indicates John's emphasis on the confession "Son of God" and away
from "Christ," thus redefining the confession "Son of God."[161]

"Sonship," as an expression of Jesus' relationship to God, was
not so evident to the people outside the circle of disciples. Jesus referred to God as *Abba* only in private instruction or personal prayer.
But even for the disciples, the extent of the meaning of Sonship seems
to stop far short of acknowledging him as God during the majority of
his ministry. Thus, "The picture which has emerged from the New
Testament . . . is clear that there has been a considerable
development over that period in early Christian belief in and under-

---

158Hengel, 66-67.

159Jack Dean Kingsbury, "The Title 'Son of God' in Matthew's Gospel," *Biblical Theology Bulletin* 5:1 (1975):3031.

160Cullmann, *Christology of the New Testament*, 279.

161James D. G. Dunn, *Unity and Diversity in the New Testament* (London:
SCM Press, Ltd., 1977), 47.

standing of Jesus as the Son of God."[162] As Longenecker explains,

> Undoubtedly the title received elaboration and extension of meaning in its use by Christians during the first century. Under the guidance of the Spirit, the Church's understanding certainly grew. But while Son of God very soon came to signify divine nature, it was probably used in a more functional manner by the earliest believers to denote Jesus' unique relationship with God the Father and his obedience to the Father's will.[163]

Marshall concurs saying, "It is a plausible argument that the primary factor in the application of the title of Son to Jesus was his status as Messiah; it was because of this status that the title of Son was originally applied to him, and only later that the title was infused with a fuller content."[164] In another place the same writer says,

> It took time for the full implications of this title to be worked out by the church. That it was connected originally with Jesus' own estimate of himself is highly probable; what the early church did was to deal out the implications of his filial consciousness, as it was confirmed by the resurrection and illuminated by Old Testament prophecy and contemporary Jewish thought. . . . the early church came to an increasing recognition of all that the title meant, so that in the end it was seen that it was not inappropriate to call Jesus "God."[165]

The later "elaboration" referred to by Longenecker is evident in John's Gospel. Cullmann writes,

> To be sure, the reserve with which Jesus speaks of his Sonship in the Synoptics disappears in John. But the reason for this is that the Paraclete who speaks through the evangelist now proclaims openly everything the disciples "could not bear" before.[166]

The turning point for the understanding of the title seems to be Jesus' passion and resurrection.[167] The most obvious demonstration

---

162Idem, *Christology in the Making*, 60.

163Longenecker, *The Christology of Early Christianity*, 98-99.

164I. Howard Marshall, "The Divine Sonship of Jesus," 99.

165Idem, *The Origins of New Testament Christology*, 123.

166Cullmann, 287.

167Paul G. Bretscher, "Exodus 4:22-23 and the Voice from Heaven," *Journal of Biblical Literature* 87 (1968):311.

of the fuller understanding of the person of Jesus is the post-resurrection confession of Thomas, "my Lord and my God" (Jn. 20:28). McDermott sees implications for a fuller understanding somewhat earlier,

> For his part Caiaphas was doubtless well-versed in Scripture and sensitive to the expectations around him, some of which . . . prepared the way for "Son of God" as a messianic title. . . . the "son" in the parable of the wicked tenants would not have escaped him; thus was his question about the "Son of the Blessed One" grounded in Scripture, tradition, and Jesus' own life and words. The post-Easter Church merely continued Caiaphas' insight into the significance of the Son of God title.[168]

Therefore, within the Gospel accounts, themselves, there is evidence for the growing recognition of the person of the Son of God. In the Synoptics it is God who first proclaims him "Son" (Mk. 1:11), but it is the Gentile centurion who recognizes him as such at his crucifixion (Mk. 15:39).[169] Kazmierski says this represents the "unfolding of God's plan . . . to understand the proclamation of Jesus' Sonship, and for that reason it is only at the end of the Gospel that the title 'Son of God' itself is presented as the unhindered proclamation of the Church and therefore no longer an obstacle to the ful-fillment of God's plan."[170]

Fennema says the Gospel of John expands the existing concept of God in explicating the "Son of God."[171] One explanation for this might be the late appearance of John's Gospel relative to the Synoptics. John thus represents more reflection on Jesus' life and more of the teaching ministry of God's Spirit.

Dunn, however, sees some evidence that the Son of God title experienced some transformation even in Matthew,

---

168McDermott, "Jesus and the Son of God Title," 305.

169By "Colwell's Rule," ("A Definite Rule for the Use of the Article in the Greek New Testament," *Journal of Biblical Literature* 52 (1933):12-21) the centurion's words cannot be taken "son of a god" but should be read "Son of God." For further discussion on this see Robert G. Bratcher, "A Note on (Mark xv. 39)," *The Expository Times* 68 (1956/57):27-28; C. F. D. Moule, *An Idiom Book of New Testament Greek* (Cambridge: Cambridge University Press, 1959), 115-16; Maximilian Zerwick, Biblical Greek, trans. and ed. Joseph Smith (Rome: Pontifical Institute, 1963), 56.

170Carl R. Kazmierski, *Jesus, the Son of God: A Study of the Markan Tradition and Its Redaction by the Evangelist* (Wurzburg: Echter Verlag, 1979), 212.

171Fennema, 296.

This Gospel was intended as something of a bridge document between a more narrowly defined Jewish Christianity on the one hand, and a Jewish Christianity much more informed by Hellenistic categories on the other. . . . Why was this? Probably because the title "Son of God" was more meaningful to a Gentile audience than Messiah could ever be. Moreover, it could serve as a good *bridge between Jewish and Gentile thought*: both societies were familiar with the idea that a good or great man might be called a son of God, and in both societies "son of God" could have connotations of divinity . . . [ital. his][172]

From the narrow culture of Palestinian Judaism to the far-reaches of the Greco-Roman world the lofty title "son of God" was known. Dunn says, "The point for us to note is that in the words of 'Jesus is the Son of God' we have a confession which had the ability to crossover cultural and national boundaries and still remain meaningful--an attribute which marks off the Son of God confession from those [such as 'Messiah' and 'Son of Man']."[173]

Yahweh would have been king over the Israelite nation (Judges 8:23; 1 Sam. 8:7). These people, however, demanded a human king to rule them (1 Sam. 8:5). Yahweh had promised that the throne of his "son" would last forever (2 Sam. 7:12-14). These concepts find culmination in the person of Jesus Christ. As the Son of God--who is both Yahweh and a man--he will sit on the throne of Israel to rule forever.

The study has pictured the Old Testament concept of sonship as three concentric circles (next page). The outermost circle represents the general meaning, the middle circle stands for the concept of "sonship to God," while the inner-most is equivalent to the sonship of Israel's king. Jesus' Sonship in the New Testament is also seen to be represented by the three circles, similar to the Old Testament because of the corresponding meanings for the term as applied to Jesus.

---

[172]Dunn, *Unity and Diversity in the New Testament*, 47.
[173]Ibid., 48.

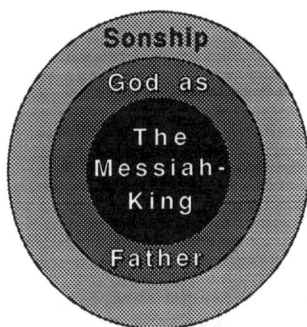

Old Testament   **New Testament**

These two sets of concentric circles might be viewed in three dimensions (below). When telescoped and fused at the common subset of the Messiah Son of God, a graphic representation of the develop-

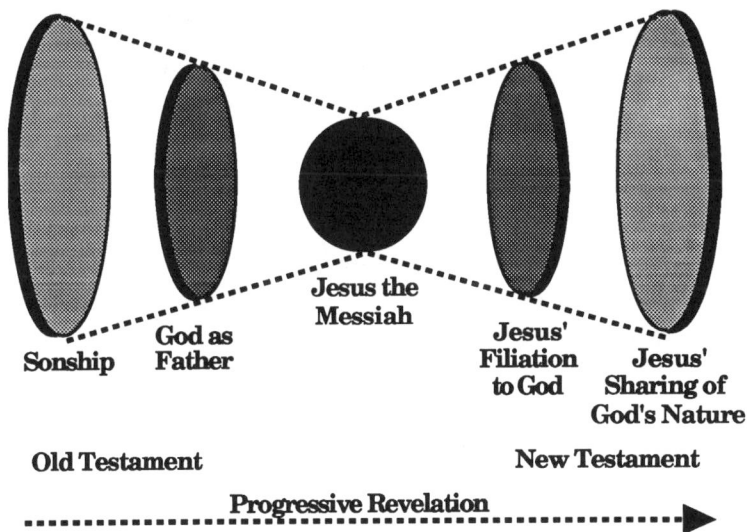

ment of the Son of God concept and the progressive nature of the revelation of the title is depicted. The concept stems from Semitic thought and Old Testament usage. It narrows when it is used to speak of Israel's relation to God, and narrows further with reference to the king as a member of the Israelite nation.

The first century A.D. Jewish expectation for the Messiah corresponded to the Old Testament king-son. But just as the Old Testament king was first a member of God's covenant people who were called his "son," so Jesus was the Messiah because he first possessed a filial relationship to God. But this Sonship entailed more than just a uniquely close relationship to God. It meant a sharing of God's essence. The understanding of this truth, however, was not so easily or so quickly comprehended. It required time for the Spirit's ministry to teach the disciples what they were not able to bear at first.

The examination portion is now complete. The study will proceed to compare the divine man Christology with the biblical title "Son of God." This comprises the second major portion of the book.

SECTION 2

REFUTATION:

THE "DIVINE MAN" AS AN EXPLANATION FOR THE NEW TESTAMENT "SON OF GOD"

This second major section will attempt to establish whether the title *theios anēr* stood behind the Christological title "Son of God." The first chapter in this section (chapter 4) will ascertain the extent to which the concept of the divine man might have affected New Testament Christology as a whole. This will be accomplished by examining the title *theios anēr* to see what diversities may have existed in the use of the term. Next, because the concept of *theios anēr* came out of Hellenism, the influence of Hellenism upon Judaism will be studied. The last part of the fourth chapter contrasts the Hellenistic and Hebraic concepts of God and man, since these have bearing on the titles *theios anēr* and "Son of God."

The final chapter will determine if the divine man concept may be seen as a valid explanation for the biblical title "Son of God." The method will be to examine the New Testament use of the term and to discover any lack of congruity between the two titles *theios anēr* and "Son of God."

4

The "Divine Man" as Background to New Testament Christology

This first chapter in the second section will seek to ascertain whether the divine man approach provides an adequate background for New Testament Christology. The chapter will compare the Hellenistic and Jewish backgrounds to the first century. The first subsection examines the variety in the use of the title "divine man."

Diversity in the "Divine Man" Concept

One of the fundamental assumptions in the divine man Christology is that the *theios anēr* was a fixed concept at the time of the writing of the New Testament. An example of this is found in Weeden's words, "Waving the red flag of the *theios anēr* Christology as he does, by introducing Jesus as the Son of God . . . Mark intends the reader to draw the only conclusion possible . . ."[1] The best example, however, comes from Bieler's definitive work. He says, "It should be an essential task of this work to show that the ancients, especially in late antiquity and early Christianity, had an identical understanding of the divine man."[2] As the following comparisons will show, there was no "identical understanding" of the concept of the divine man.

An analysis of Bieler's work, which has had the most marked impact in shaping the divine man Christology, shows it to be deeply flawed. Of Bieler's study Morton Smith says, "But (as in Wetter's work) secondary factors diminished the impact of the book: it was somewhat careless; the references were sometimes false and the texts sometimes misinterpreted; the choice of sources was questionable."[3] Goppelt adds, "The material was collected without the neces-

---

[1]Theodore J. Weeden, "The Heresy That Necessitated Mark's Gospel," *Zeitschrift für neutestamentliche Wissenschaft* 59 (1968):148.

[2]Ludwig Bieler, *ΘΕΙΟΣ ΑΝΗΡ*, 1:145. See Appendix for the German quote.

[3]Morton Smith, "Prolegomena to a Discussion of Aretalogies, Divine Men, the Gospels and Jesus," *Journal of Biblical Literature* 90 (1970):192.

sary critical stratification by L. Bieler."[4]

Bieler's use of "questionable sources" is evident in his tendency to put much weight on writings which came centuries after the time of Christ. For example, he refers to Iamblichus' *Life of Pythagoras* (fourth century A.D.) to substantiate the commonality of birth announcements of divine men.[5] His tendency to collect the material without "critical stratification" is also seen in this example. Bieler goes on to speak of this sort of announcement as part of the divine man portrait but fails to mention that the term *theios anēr* is absent from Iamblichus' writing at this point.

For all of Bieler's efforts to link the *theios anēr* concept to the title "Son of God," he does not offer one citation from ancient literature in which these two titles are specifically linked. Even so, when examining the use of in the Gospels, he does not hesitate to call it a "Hellenistic trait."[6] Although he was aware that there were a variety of characteristics of the various divine men, Bieler believed that each of the representatives possessed these characteristics to some extent.[7] He discounts these divergences as only mere "shadings" of the image of the "ideal divine man."[8]

One of the most helpful recent works on the topic of the divine man is *The Charismatic Figure as Miracle Worker*.[9] In this study Tiede says the divergences between the various types of divine men are too sharp to be discounted as Bieler does.[10] As von Martitz says, "The generous use of *theios anēr* in Bieler gives the wrong idea that there was a designation and fixed concept in this early period."[11] As shall be seen later in this section, no such common designation or fixed concept was present during the time of Christ.

After gathering information which spanned centuries, Bieler tended to make sweeping generalizations. Some individuals who were said to have attained divine status supposedly exhibited knowl-

---

[4]Leonhard Goppelt, *Theology of the New Testament*, trans. John E. Alsup (Grand Rapids: Wm. B. Eerdmans, 1982), 2:70, n. 8.

[5]Bieler, 1:23.

[6]Ibid., 139.

[7]Ibid., 4.

[8]Ibid., 143.

[9]W. L. Liefeld says in "The Hellenistic 'Divine Man' and the Figure of Jesus in the Gospels," *Journal of the Evangelical Theological Society* 16 (1973):197, that Tiede's work is so important that "all *theios aner* theories henceforth [must] be judged by it."

[10]David Lenz Tiede, *The Charismatic Figure as Miracle Worker* (Missoula, MT: Scholars Press, 1972), 59.

[11]*Theological Dictionary of the New Testament*, s.v. "υἱός," by Peter Wülfing von Martitz, 8 (1972):338.

edge without being taught. Bieler saw this to be a trait of the *theios anēr*.[12] Other characteristic features included perfect obedience to God, the presence of life-threatening adversaries, the working of miracles and a martyr's death.[13] The problem for Bieler is that few examples are linked specifically to the title *theios anēr*. Concerning this tendency to generalize Tiede says,

> Bieler aggregated so many features into his composite portrait of the "typical divine man" that it would be difficult to find any hero in antiquity to whom at least several of these qualities were not attributed, and it is perhaps as difficult to find a pre-third century A.D. portrayal of any figure which supplies its hero with Bieler's complete catalog of the characteristics of the "divine man." . . . Thus once again, the diversity that was recognized in the sources was treated by Bieler as of secondary importance compared with the general conception of the "divine man" which he believed he could identify in a wide variety of contexts.[14]

On this great diversity which Bieler saw as unimportant, Otto Betz comments,

> The "divine man" type seems to me to be an artificial construction . . . Anyone who is not blinded by the mass of material in Bieler's book will easily see, that it does not always fit the "divine man" type very well. The designation appears only rarely, and individual miraculous features do not make up a particular homogenous type.[15]

Thus Bieler tended to aggregate many features from a plethora of individuals referred to in ancient literature into one composite divine man. But no such *theios anēr* could actually be found depicted in any one piece of literature. On this von Martitz observes,

> θεῖος ἀνήρ is by no means a fixed expression at least in the pre-Christian era. θεῖος is mostly used predicatively. Some are called θεῖος without any ascription of a charismatic character, while others have this character but never in the tradition are called

---

[12]Bieler, 1:35.

[13]Ibid., 39-44.

[14]Tiede, 246-47.

[15]Otto Betz, *What Do We Know about Jesus?* (Philadelphia: The Westminster Press, 1968), 64.

θεῖος.[16]

Much diversity existed in the use of the the term θεῖος, therefore. In fact the term transcended the confined use of "divine" and was often employed with reference to the performance of magic or even sorcery. Liefeld explains,

> [In the age of Hellenism] the same wonderful deed might be interpreted by some as a miracle and by others as magic. The performer of the deed might, therefore, be considered on one hand as *theios* and on the other as a *magus* [magician] or a *goēs* [sorcerer]. This fact, and the variety of figures who were considered divine for different reasons . . . should guard us against making the facile assumption that there was a general type honored as a *theios anēr*.[17]

In general, there are just too many figures and too many features associated with the term *theios anēr* to assume a composite figure. Concerning this Morton Smith says,

> The development of the "divine man" figure in the Graeco-Roman world was part and parcel of the general development of that world's imaginations and desires. . . . One can distinguish roughly the different social types of those who claimed or were credited with divinity--prophets, poets, philosophers, rulers, athletes, physicians, magicians . . . But there are too many borderline cases and too many tie-ins from one type to another.[18]

Consequently, as Klaus Berger points out, "divine man" must be thought of as a collection of abstracts and is unsuited for use as a fixed concept.[19] Howard Kee asserts, "There is no set type or model of θεῖος ἀνήρ."[20]

Recognizing the extent of the diversity, H. D. Betz says, "the concept of the Divine Man is open to considerable variation."[21] In the

---

[16]Von Martitz, 339.

[17]Liefeld, 199.

[18]Smith, 186-87.

[19]Klaus Berger, "Zum Problem der Messianität Jesu," *Zeitschrift fur Theologie und Kirche* 71 (1974):6.

[20]Howard Clark Kee, *Jesus in History: An Approach to the Study of the Gospels* (New York: Harcourt, Brace & World, Inc., 1970), 134.

[21]Hans Dieter Betz, "Jesus as Divine Man," in *Jesus and the Historian*, ed. F. Thomas Trotter (Philadelphia: The Westminster Press, 1968), 116.

same article, Betz later attempts to narrow that variation somewhat when he states, "The Gospels and their source materials represent five different versions of the Divine Man Christology."[22] In response to this statement Tiede says, "'The Divine Man Christology' . . . would have to be too broad a concept to have much specific interpretative value."[23]

Perhaps the chief pitfall in Bieler's method, as Holladay puts it, is his "indiscriminately crossing chronological boundaries."[24] Although Bieler does cite some examples from pre-Christian literature, Hengel points out that the overwhelming majority of his sources come from Neo-Platonism and the church's hagiography.[25] This methodology is also used by Gillis Wetter in *Der Sohn Gottes*. He bases his general conception of the divine man on literature from the second and third centuries A.D. He then links these with the Gospel portrayal of Jesus.[26] An historical survey shows more graphically the diversity of the divine man picture.

Tiede notes how the use of the term *theios* began to be applied variously during the time of Plato. Whereas the term had some religious connotations, Plato began to employ the term to depict the ideal philosopher.[27] Alongside this grew the tradition of the *theios anēr* as the shaman who worked wonders to manifest the divine presence.[28] But this latter aspect of the divine man's activities was not so prevalent before the time of Christ. Eduard Schweizer says that it is an anachronism to attempt to apply a fixed divine man concept to writings of the first century A.D.[29] Elsewhere Schweizer says,

It is doubtful whether the concept of a Hellenistic "divine man" in the sense it is always used, ever existed before the middle of the second century A.D. Before that, the term designated poets,

---

[22]Ibid., 129.

[23]Tiede, 265, n. 63.

[24]Carl R. Holladay, *Theios Aner in Hellenistic Judaism: A Critique of the Use of this Category in New Testament Christology* (Missoula, MT: Scholars Press, 1977), 18.

[25]Martin Hengel, *The Son of God*, trans. John Bowden (Philadelphia: Fortress Press, 1976), 31.

[26]Gillis Wetter, *Der Sohn Gottes. Eine Untersuchung über den Character und die Tendenz des Johannes-evangeliums.* (Göttingen: Vandenhoeck & Ruprecht, 1916), 71.

[27]Tiede, 30.

[28]Eric Robertson Dodds, *The Greeks and the Irrational* (Berkeley: University of California Press, 1959), 135-46.

[29]Eduard Schweizer, *Jesus*, trans. D. E. Green (London: SCM Press, 1971), 127, n. 10.

artists, statesmen, and philosophers.[30]

Tiede's in-depth study traces the gradual change which occurred in the picture of the divine man,

> It is perhaps possible to take a barometric reading of the changing cultural climate of this phase of the Hellenistic period by comparing the perspectives on this point represented by Plutarch and Seneca in the first century [A.D.], Lucian [of Samosata] in the second, and Philostratus and Porphyry in the third . . . Plutarch and Seneca confidently display the divine sage Socrates and his moral courage in the face of death in order to dismiss attempts to authenticate figures as divine on the basis of miraculous displays. Lucian is fighting on several fronts in an attempt to maintain this criterion, but the growth and convergence of the cults of such figures as Peregrinus and Alexander show he is fighting a bitter and losing battle against popular response. Philostratus and Porphyry, by contrast, appear to have made peace with Lucian's opposition; and although they are still aware of the philosophical standard, they maintain that Apollonius and Pythagoras were divine by describing their heroes as both sages and miracle workers.[31]

Tiede's study shows that even in the third century the philosophical and wisdom aspect of the divine man figure yet remains. Walter Burkert demonstrates that the Neo-Pythagoreans (second century A.D.) were divided over seeing their founder as a shaman or a great scientist.[32] Even H. D. Betz admits that at the time of Lucian of Samosata in the second century the *theios anēr* was "not clearly defined."[33]

In summary, this section has demonstrated the fatal flaws of the divine man Christology due to its lack of critical differentiation between the various types of figures called 'divine.' For the most part, this has been the result of indiscriminately collecting various characteristics of those called *theioi* and then viewing this conglomerate

---

[30]Idem, "Towards a Christology of Mark?" in *God's Christ and His People, Studies in Honor of Nils Alstrup Dahl.* ed. Jacob Jervell and Wayne A. Meeks (Oslo, Norway: Universitetsforlaget, 1977), 30.

[31]Tiede, 98-99.

[32]Walter Burkert, *Weisheit und Wissenschaft* Nürnberg: Verlag Hans Carl, 98-150.

[33]"Terminologisch ist der θεῖος ἀνήρ bei Lukian nicht fest umrissen." Hans Dieter Betz, *Lukian von Samosata und das Neue Testament* (Berlin: Akademie-Verlag, 1961), 102.

picture as the archtypical divine man. As Otto Betz says,

> I think we have to go further and raise the question whether there really existed the concept of such a Divine Man, whether one can speak of him as a generally known "type" composed of distinguishable features. . . . In Hellenistic writings, the adjective *theios* is used quite frequently . . . But the term *theios anēr* is quite rare. . . . therefore I wonder whether we should speak of a Hellenistic "Divine Man" . . . Hellenists knew many *theioi*, but they did not develop a concept and type *theios anēr*.[34]

In assessing this issue, William Lane is even more emphatic. He states,

> But no appeal may be made to some fixed norm in Hellenism which permits the general designation "divine man Christology" as an explanation for a particular motif or perspective. The generalized portrait of the *theios anēr* presupposed in modern critical studies of the gospel tradition must be recognized as a synthetic construct which fails to make the differentiations demanded by the primary sources.[35]

Nevertheless, there were instances when charismatic figures were termed *theios anēr*. The issue becomes why and when. Apparently, as it was occasionally used, there occurred a gradual change in the application of the term. Its application with reference to miracle-workers does not appear until the latter half of the second century A.D. As Lane points out,

> The [Hellenistic] texts . . . demonstrate that the basis upon which a figure was authenticated as divine was not a matter of indifference to Hellenistic literary authors. The diverse attempts in the Hellenistic world to authenticate the divine stature or power of a charismatic figure can be identified, and the criteria which were employed to evaluate such claims can still be distinguished. In the educated and literary stratum of Greco-Roman culture prior to the mid-second century A.D., the vitality

---

34Otto Betz, "The Concept of the So-Called 'Divine Man' in Mark's Christology," in *Studies in New Testament and Early Christian Literature*, ed. David Edward Aune (Leiden: E. J. Brill, 1972), 232.

35William Lane, *"Theios Aner* Christology and the Gospel of Mark," in *New Dimensions in New Testament Study*, ed. Richard N. Longenecker and Merrill Tenney (Grand Rapids: Zondervan Publishing House, 1974), 147.

of a carefully cultivated image of the ideal wise man, whose life and death displayed his divine moral excellence, provided a criterion by which appeal to teratological accounts could be resisted. In popular circles this discrimination tended to break down; and . . . after the mid-second century A.D., appeals to miraculous or magical displays of power to authenticate figures as divine become increasingly common.[36]

What then of the divine man conception which some see behind the description of Jesus in the New Testament? Many of the figures referred to as "divine" in Hellenistic literature come not from pre-Christian times, but actually follow the time of Christ. Wetter's references to Hellenistic figures in *Der Sohn Gottes* which he saw as paralleling the Gospel portrait of Jesus came from literature of the second and third centuries A.D. This prompted Tiede to say, "it was perhaps more valuable as a study of the way gospel traditions were used by the apologists."[37] Prümm suggests that the miracle stories attributed to the Hellenistic divine men are often deliberate plagarisms from the gospel accounts.[38]

It seems unlikely, therefore, that first century Hellenists, let alone Palestinian Jews, would have been receptive to the proclamation of Jesus as the "divine man." Gundry points out that it is erroneous to think that, "as the tradition concerning Jesus moved out into the wider Hellenistic world, aretalogists spun miracle stories around him in order to portray him as a miracle-working divine man. For in literary circles of the first century, Hellenistic divine men gained authentication from their exemplification of moral virtue."[39]

Some may yet insist that the miracle-working divine man concept possibly could have existed among the Hellenistic populace, though not present in the literature. Because Jesus lived and ministered first to the Jews, and because most divine men advocates see the concept entering the church via Hellenistic Judaism, the effect of Hellenism upon Judaism requires examination.

The Hellenistic Influence on Judaism

The necessity for this section is explained by Carl Holladay in his

---

[36]Ibid., 146.

[37]Tiede, 244.

[38]K. Prümm, *Religionsgeschichte Handbuch* (Rome: Päpstliches Bibelinstitut, 1954), 458-64.

[39]Robert H. Gundry, "Recent Investigations into the Literary Genre 'Gospel,'" in *New Dimensions in New Testament Study*, 108.

Theios Anēr in Hellenistic Judaism. He shows that the divine man
Christology has developed "a fairly clearly defined position"[40] which
includes the following: 1) within the Hellenistic world the *theios anēr*
was a wide-spread and popularly known figure; 2) within Jewish life
and thought as reflected in the Old Testament, the notion of a "divine
man" was inconsistent with the "men of God" such as priests, prophets and kings; 3) within Jewish thought due to the impact of
Hellenization, a transformation took place as Hellenistic Jews began
to reinterpret their ancient heroes to conform to the Hellenistic *theios
anēr* image, so that by the first century A.D. it was not uncommon
for Jews to perceive certain Old Testament figures as divine men;
4) this change within Hellenistic Judaism made possible the concep-
tualization of Jesus in this vein, especially where Hellenistic Judaism was more dominant.[41]

To ascertain whether this thesis is correct, one needs to consider
the Jewish situation in Palestine following the exile. John Bright
says of this period,

> The religion of the post-exilic period is marked by a tremendous
> concern for the keeping of the law . . . This is indeed its dis-
> tinctive characteristic and that which more than anything else,
> distinguishes it from the religion of pre-exilic Israel. This does
> not mean that it was a new religion, or represented the importa-
> tion of some strange new element to Israel's faith. Rather, it
> resulted from a heightened stress . . . [42]

Bright goes on to say,

> Judaism tended to draw apart from the world . . . the commun-
> ity had to fight for its identity as "Israel" over against . . . others
> resident in the land whose religious purity was dubious. . . .
> Lines had to be drawn sharply if the community was not simply
> to dissolve into its environment, losing its distinctive character
> . . . Such an ideal could never be realized if Jews began to mix
> with foreigners or become too tolerably ready to assimilate with
> them. The problem before the community was never in practice
> one of finding a strategy for implementing the world-wide
> implications of its faith, but of standing clear of the world in
> order to protect its identity . . . Indeed, the community's whole
> history, culminating in the Maccabean crisis, showed clearly

---

[40]Holladay, 15.
[41]Ibid., 15-17.
[42]John Bright, *A History of Israel*, 430.

that it must be separate, be Jewish, or consent to the disappearance of Judaism as a distinctive entity.[43]

Martin Hengel shows how the literature reflects Jewish separatism,

Thus the terminology of 2 Maccabees is very significant. The Jews seem to have felt the new Greek way of life to be an "aggressive" civilization which threatened to alienate them from the distinctive tradition of their fathers.[44]

As a result of this separationistic spirit, Zvi Cahn says, "Hellenism was never able to gain a solid foothold in the land during the era of the Second Temple."[45] Thus Palestinian Judaism was able to "preserve their traditional religious heritage."[46]

Hengel's extensive study on the impact of the Hellenistic culture on Judaism as a whole prompts him to say that "Hellenism . . . has a very strong political and social element. Compared with that . . . its philosophical, literary and religious impact was of secondary importance."[47] This observation is substantiated in the writings of Hellenistic Jewish authors. Otto Betz points out,

It would be silly to deny the fact that the Jews dispersed in the Roman Empire and even those living in Palestine were part of the Hellenistic culture, it is also true that the religion of the Hebrews was not immersed in the melting pot of Hellenistic syncretism. . . . Jewish apocalypticism, the writings of Qumran, and the literature of the rabbis are essentially different from both Greek philosophy and Hellenistic religions.[48]

The modern development of the divine man Christology holds that Hellenistic philosophical and religious categories did impact Judaism, and this impact is demonstrable in authors such as Philo and Josephus. Paul Achtemeier says, for example, "The description

---

[43]Ibid., 443-444.

[44]Martin Hengel, *Jews, Greeks and Barbarians*, trans. John Bowden (Philadelphia: Fortress Press, 1980), 78.

[45]Zvi Cahn, *The Philosophy of Judaism* (New York: The Macmillan Company, 1962), 11.

[46]Hengel, *Jews, Greeks, and Barbarians*, 125.

[47]Ibid., 67.

[48]Otto Betz, "The Concept of the So-Called 'Divine Man' in Mark's Christology," in *Studies in New Testament and Early Christian Literature*, 233.

of Moses in Josephus, and especially Philo, indicates the attempt to
make him appear a *theios anēr*, complete with all the virtues of such
a figure, and miracle-working is then also a part of the role of the
expected 'one like Moses.'"[49] But Tiede militates against this saying,
"Although . . . Philo is seeking ways to document the reliability of the
biblical account, [his writings] do not demonstrate that the miracles
provide a primary basis for Philo to authenticate Moses as a 'divine
man.'"[50] W. D. Davies says of Philo's writings,

> But often the philosophical terminology, which Philo is com-
> pelled to use for his purpose, obscures the similarity of his reli-
> gion with that expressed so naively in the literature of Palestine
> Jewry. . . . The mode by which he thought to come into contact
> with God was Greek, but the God with whom he desired to come
> into contact was the God of Israel.[51]

More specifically Kee states,

> In Jewish literature of the Graeco-Roman period, Moses is
> portrayed as agent of God, whose divine enablement empowers
> him to perform extraordinary deeds. But . . . there is no effort to
> picture Moses as a divinized man . . . In [Philo's] portrayal of
> Moses as king--just as in Josephus' representation of Moses and
> other patriarchs of ancient Israel--Philo's intent is to show that
> they exemplified the wisdom of the truly virtuous man or the
> wise ruler of the Cynic and Stoic philosophical traditions. Both
> maintain a clear distinction between the human and the divine.
> . . . It is unwarranted, therefore, to assume that there was in
> Hellenistic Judaism a paradigmatic figure of a divinized mir-
> acle-worker to which the early Christian image of Jesus was
> made to conform . . .[52]

The most damaging blow to this aspect of the divine man theory
(that the concept came first via Hellenistic Judaism to the Hellenistic-Jewish church) comes from the work of Carl Holladay. Kee says
of Holladay's *Theios Anēr in Hellenistic Judaism* that it "subjected to

---

49Paul J. Achtemeier, "The Origin and Function of the Pre Markan Miracle
Catenae," *Journal of Biblical Literature* 91 (1972):202.

50Tiede, 134.

51W. D. Davies, *Paul and Rabbinic Judaism*, fourth edition (Philadelphia:
Fortress Press, 1980), 12.

52Howard Kee, "Mark's Gospel in Recent Research,"*Interpretation* 32 (1978):
360.

painstaking analysis the key works of Josephus, Philo and Artapanus bearing on their use of θεός, θεῖος and θεῖος ἀνήρ with the aim of determining what the term θεῖος ἀνήρ means for these writers."[53] In this well-documented study Holladay concludes that 1) none of these writers depicted Moses or any other Old Testament hero as deified; 2) rather, their apologetics actually widen the gap between God and man; 3) the propagandizing efforts of Hellenistic Jews did not lead them to stress miracle traditions; 4) the real agent of the miracles is always God and never a *theios aner*; 5) the miracle tradition of Hellenistic Judaism is in continuity with the salvation history of the Old Testament rather than pagan Hellenism.[54] The findings of Holladay's definitive study substantiates I. H. Marshall's claim that there really is "no evidence for a separate Hellenistic Gentile church and theology in the early period . . ."[55]

In particular, with regard to Philo's use of the term *theios aner*, Holladay says,

> On the basis of the foregoing analysis of his use of such language, especially with its focus upon the *nous/psychē,* it is untenable simply to treat the claims of Empedocles and Apollonius together with Philo's statements about Moses without noticing, and respecting, the vast difference between the respective points of view. To wrench passages from their context in Philo and lift them from his complex and often incoherent system of thought only serves to complicate and distort an already complicated picture, and above all, results in attributing to Philo convictions and beliefs at which he would be appalled.[56]

Holladay says that basically, "Philo seems deliberately to avoid the use of *theios aner,* and the application of *theios* to individuals."[57]

Although few would argue that a narrow and separatistic Judaism existed in Palestine during the period of Jesus' life, evidence points to a fidelity of Jewish theology by Hellenistic Jews, also. The rationale for this may lie in the fact that the synagogue was found wherever there were Jews throughout the Diaspora. This pro-

[53]Idem, *Community of the New Age: Studies in Mark's Gospel* (Philadelphia: The Westminster Press, 1977), 185, n. 72.

[54]Holladay, 233-42. Cf. Kee, *Community of the New Age* (Philadelphia: The Westminster Press, 1977), 185, n. 72.

[55]I. Howard Marshall, "Palestinian and Hellenistic Christianity: Some Critical Comments," *New Testament Studies* 19 (1973):286.

[56]Holladay, 197.

[57]Ibid., 196.

vided a place for regular worship and the reading and exposition of the law.[58] The strength of this fellowship, and the regular exposure and contemplation of the Scriptures, helped keep Judaism pure.

Another argument used by divine man adherents is the obvious influence of Hellenistic miracle stories upon Jewish writing and the Gospels. This literature, it is contended, was a well-known genre contemporary with the New Testament. Achtemeier asserts that the miracle stories of the New Testament "belong, in content and style, to the age in which they originated."[59] To support this statement he offers examples from the Babylonian Talmud where rabbi's prayers bring about miraculous events.[60] Helmut Koester says,

> Aretalogies were normally written for purposes of religious propaganda. The religious convictions which incline to the use of this literary genre . . . are very much the same everywhere in the Hellenistic world, whether they be Jewish, pagan or Christian.[61]

Koester then offers as an example "the typical ending of an aretalogy in Sir. 43:27-29 and 1 Macc. 9:22."[62]

In response to Koester's citations, Kee says, "The irony lies in the fact that in neither of these texts [Sirach or 1 Maccabees] is there the slightest hint of a divine man concept . . ."[63] Walter Schmithals responds to Achtemeier's reference to rabbinic literature by pointing out that rabbinic miracles are always performed through the power of prayer to God rather than because the rabbi himself has the ability to effect them.[64]

Moreover, Kee shows the fallacy in speaking of aretalogy as a particular genre in Hellenistic literature. There is too much diversity of materials to categorize them under one heading.[65] Furthermore, although pre-canonical collections of miracles concerning Jesus may

---

[58]Bright, 437.

[59]Shirley Jackson Case calls it "a miracle-loving age," *The Origins of Christian Supernaturalism* (Chicago: The University of Chicago Press, 1946), vi.

[60]Paul J. Achtemeier, "Gospel Miracle Tradition and the Divine Man," *Interpretation* 26 (1972):184.

[61]Helmut Koester, "One Jesus and Four Primitive Gospels," in *Trajectories through Early Christianity* (Philadelphia: Fortress Press, 1971), 188.

[62]Ibid.

[63]Howard Clark Kee, *Community of the New Age*, 24.

[64]Walter Schmithals, *Wunder und Glaube. Eine Auslegung von Markus 4,35-6,6a* (Neukirchen: Neukirchener Verlag, 1970), 20.

[65]Howard Clark Kee, "Aretalogy and Gospel," *Journal of Biblical Literature* 92 (1973):402-22.

have occurred, it is too presumptuous to assume that pagan parallels in Hellenism indicate that the same sort of apotheosis is occurring in the Gospels.[66] This is because the Gospels cannot be considered to fit into any tradition of literature found in Hellenism.[67] Amos Wilder goes so far as to say that the Gospels represent a whole new literary genre.[68]

The Judaism of the first century, and therefore the Gospels, cannot be seen to be a part of a Hellenistic stream. As Barr points out, the efforts to understand the New Testament in light of its contextual setting, of parallels in other literature and currents of tradition is of little help, for "in the end . . . biblical study itself . . . would be freer without it."[69] When the text is permitted to speak for itself, Longenecker says, "It is becoming increasingly evident today that in the scientific study of the New Testament, the Jewish backgrounds rather than the Grecian parallels offer the soundest basis of approach."[70] As Nicol says, the problem in seeing Hellenistic legends behind New Testament miracle accounts is that "many of the New Testament miracle stories bear such clearly Jewish features that it is difficult to see how they could have been inspired by the purely pagan *theios anēr*-concept."[71]

To summarize this section, it seems clear that Judaism, not only in the area of Palestine but also in the Diaspora, maintained its distinction from certain Hellenistic influences. The social, economic, and to some extent even the philosophical aspects of Hellenism made their mark on the Jews. But this was necessary for the people's existence and for an effective apologetic of their faith. The appeal by some to the working of miracles in rabbinic and Hellenistic Jewish works only reinforces the presence of the Jewish tradition. The great men of God in the Old Testament often performed miracles by the power of God. As in the Old Testament, these miracles pointed to God's ability rather than to man's. As Otto Betz notes, the Septuagint did not render the Hebrew "man of God" by *theios anēr*, which it probably would have if this term had been a common designation for a well-known concept in the Hellenistic world and if the Jews had

---

[66]Ibid.

[67]Kee, "Mark's Gospel in Recent Research," 364.

[68]Amos Wilder, *Early Christian Rhetoric: The Language of the Gospel* (Cambridge, MA: Harvard University Press, 1964), 36.

[69]*Interpreter's Dictionary of the Bible*, Supplementary Volume, s.v. "Biblical Theology," by James Barr, 110.

[70]Richard N. Longenecker, *The Christology of Early Jewish Christianity* (Naperville, IL: Alec R. Allenson Inc.,1970), 24.

[71]W. Nicol, *The Semeia in the Fourth Gospel: Tradition and Redaction* (Leiden: E. J. Brill, 1972), 49.

been affected as such by Hellenism.[72]

One more area of investigation remains in this chapter. The following section examines the differences between the way the Greeks and the Jews viewed God and man.

The Hellenistic versus the Hebraic Concepts of God and Man

If any similitude of Jewish tradition does stand behind the writing of the New Testament (and the Gospels in particular), then one of the major difficulties in the divine man Christology is the lack of recognition of the difference between the Hellenistic and Hebraic views of God and man. Of Bieler's study Holladay says,

> The fundamental differences between the Hellenistic and the Biblical thought-worlds stand in an uneasy, and in some respects, an unresolved tension throughout the work. The historical and conceptual continuity of the Old Testament and New Testament, and the discontinuity of both of these to Hellenistic thought (and Far Eastern thought) calls for some explanation by Bieler in view of the fact that all three traditions [are said by Bieler to] yield essentially identical formal portraits of the *theios anēr* personality within their respective traditions.[73]

But an identical portrait of the *theios anēr* is shown not to be the case when Judaism and Hellenism are compared. As Nicol states, "In pure Jewish thought, there was a clear separation between God and man, but this was not the case in Hellenistic thought, where nearly all extraordinary men such as sages, statesmen, prophets, and wonder workers were seen as partly divine, as *theioi andres*."[74]

For Israel, God was a being of moral perfection and world-transcending majesty, who must necessarily keep himself separate from the sinful impurity of human living.[75] Israel's God was "absolutely superior over nature."[76] Concerning the Jewish view of Yahweh's relation to the world, Von Rad says,

---

[72]Otto Betz, "The Concept of the So-Called 'Divine Man' in Mark's Christology," in *Studies in New Testament and Early Christian Literature*, 332-33.

[73]Holladay, 31.

[74]W. Nicol, 48.

[75]Walther Eichrodt, *Theology of the Old Testament*, trans. J. A. Baker (Philadelphia: Westminster Press), 2:373.

[76]Ibid., 74.

However powerful his sway in it was, theologically he still transcended it. Nature was not a mode of Yahweh's being; he stood over against it as its creator.[77]

But this was not just the picture of God in the Old Testament. This was the view which post-exilic Judaism held of their God. W. D. Davies says. "One of the marks of post-exilic Judaism is an increasing emphasis on what has been called the 'Transcendence of God.'"[78] Davies goes on to say, "The meticulous scrupulosity of the Law and the extreme punctiliousness with which the approach to God by sacrifice and in worship was regulated have been regarded as proofs of the extreme transcendentalism of the post-exilic idea of God."[79] Hengel says this meticulous emphasis on the Law was, at least in part, a reaction to what the Jews perceived in Hellenism to be "an aggressive civilization which threatened to alienate them from the distinctive tradition of their fathers."[80] Consequently, and in contrast with the Greeks, the God of the Jews forbade any divinization of men.[81] The nature of the transcendent Yahweh could not be confused with that of sinful man whose tendency it was to drift further from God into sin.[82]

Yet many adherents of the divine man Christology see the Greek concepts of God and man (which is seen as part and parcel of the *theios anēr* conception[83]) to have entered the Gospels via Hellenistic Judaism. After his detailed study of the writings of Philo, Josephus and Artapanus, Holladay concludes,

As to the question of whether in Hellenistic-Judaism it became easier for Jews to conceive of a divine man because the line of demarcation between man and God had become blurred, we have seen evidence that suggests that Hellenization among Jews, rather than bridging the gap, only widened it. As surprizing as it may sound, Philo offers the best proof of this--the radical dualism between Creator and creature, between God and

---

[77]Gerhard von Rad, *Old Testament Theology*, trans. D. M. G. Stalker (New York: Harper & Row, 1962), 1:218.

[78]Davies, 164.

[79]Ibid., 177.

[80]Hengel, 78.

[81]Ibid.

[82]Eichrodt, 2:389. Cf. Gen. 6:5; 8:21; Isa. 5:18; 9:18; Jer. 2:23, 25; 6:7; 13:23; 17:9; Ezek. 16:48, 51; 23:11; 36:26.

[83]Ferdinand Hahn, *The Titles of Jesus in Christology*, trans. Harold Knight and George Ogg (New York: World Publishing Company, 1969), 289.

man, if anything became more deeply entrenched in Philo.[84]

The New Testament also presents God the Father in this light. He is the one who is infathomable (Matt. 11:25) and unapproachable by any other means than through Jesus (Jn. 14:6).

The Greeks, on the other hand, saw God and man quite differently. Unlike the God of Israel who is superior to and apart from the creation, the God of the Greeks is an integral part of nature. Bultmann says, "Greek thought always regards God in the last analysis as a part of the world or as identical with the world, even when, or rather especially when, he is held to be the origin and formative cosmic principle which lies beyond the world of phenomena. . . . Greek thought tends therefore to pantheism . . ."[85] Concerning this pantheism Kleinknecht says,

> God and the cosmos are identical. . . . A philosophical concept of God [arises which is] pantheistic and full of belief in providence . . . it banishes or refashions all personal features from the conception of God . . . by way of in man there followed increasingly an "inwardizing" of the concept of God in us.[86]

The Greeks also viewed man quite differently than did the Jews. Morton Smith states, "Philosophy--and especially Plato whose influence was all-pervasive--popularized the notion that man is composed of a divine soul imprisoned in a material body; thus every man is essentially divine, and those whose souls are most powerful or who subjugate their bodies completely are almost present deities."[87] Bultmann says of the Greek's view of man,

> With the decline of the city state, the Greek view of life underwent further modification at the hands of the Stoics. . . . The universal law is the law of [man's] own being. Man has his own appropriate place in a universe of which he himself is a part. . . . Thus the universe is a living organism with a soul . . . Indeed, it is the deity itself. . . . Man is essentially a Logos-being. It is important for him to recognize his identity with the universal

---

[84]Holladay, 235.

[85]Rudolf Bultmann, Jesus and the Word, trans. Louise Pettibone Smith and Ermine Huntress Lantero (New York: Charles Scribner's Sons, 1958), 134.

[86]Theological Dictionary of the New Testament, s.v. "θεός," by Hermann Kleinknecht, 3 (1965):75.

[87]Morton Smith, "Prolegomena to a Discussion of Aretalogies, Divine Men, and Gospels and Jesus," 182.

Logos . . . [which] must hold the reins of government in him if he is to achieve his end, which is happiness . . . his life must be lived as a unity . . . This, however, means "being at one with nature" . . . for the individual Logos is also the universe Logos of nature.[88]

In Greek thought there was a widespread idea that the human soul comes down to earth to a body from a heavenly home.[89] Man, therefore, is in a state of tension. He is not a specific species of being,[90] but hovers between the two poles of the lofty divine and the base animal.[91] Bultmann says, "The spirit dwelling in the body is . . . identical with the universal Logos . . . It is the divine element in him."[92]

How does the divine man fit into this picture? He is the one who, according to Hans Dieter Betz, is "man in the full sense; then his humanity becomes the epiphany of the divine."[93] Lane adds, "The term *theios anēr* describes the exceptionally gifted and extraordinary individual whose command of a higher, revelational wisdom and of a divine power displays that the tension experienced by other men has been resolved by the increasing dominance of the divine aspect of human nature."[94]

In summary, it is clear that for the Hellenist "God and man are one by nature."[95] This could never approximate the Jewish view of God and man. In Hellenism there was a tendency to make men into gods and gods to be like men.[96] Hengel points out that the Stoics proclaimed that all men are children of Zeus by nature because they bear his seed since they have the ability to reason.[97] The Jews could

---

[88]Rudolf Bultmann, *Primitive Christianity in Its Contemporary Setting*, trans. R. H. Fuller (New York: Meridian Books, 1957), 135-36, 142.

[89]Arthur Darby Nock, *Essays on Religion and the Ancient World*, ed. Zeph Stewart (Oxford: Clarendon Press, 1972), 2:840.

[90]Hans Dieter Betz, "Jesus as the Divine Man," 116.

[91]*Die Religion in Geschichte und Gegenwart*, s.v. "Mensch," by C. H. Ratchow (Tübingen: J. C. B. Mohr), 4:860-61.

[92]Bultmann, *Primitive Christianity in the Contemporary Setting*, 142.

[93]H. D. Betz, "Jesus as the Divine Man," 116.

[94]William Lane, "Theios Aner Christology and the Gospel of Mark," in *New Dimensions in New Testament Study*, ed. Richard N. Longenecker and Merrill Tenney (Grand Rapids: Zondervan Publishing House, 1974), 146.

[95]*Theological Dictionary of the New Testament*, s.v. "παῖς," by Albrecht Oepke, 5 (1967):652.

[96]C. H. Dodd, *The Interpretation of the Fourth Gospel* (Cambridge: The University Press, 1968), 251.

[97]Hengel goes on to say that this view led to the assumption that a "son of God"

never picture their creator and covenant God in this manner.[98] Israel's God was necessarily separate from human sinfulness.[99] Their God's holiness, purity, and transcendence caused them to see him as standing against creation.[100] He was never considered a part of it in any pantheistic sense. As Cullmann remarks, "The Hellenistic concept is so deeply rooted in polytheistic thought that it can hardly be transferred to a monotheistic framework."[101] Edwards says,

> The Hellenistic doctrine of the soul, which forms the root of the "divine man" in Hellenism, stands fundamentally opposed to a Jewish understanding of the relationship between man and God. The divine soul which is imprisoned in each man according to Greek thought finds little accomodation in Judaism where man is not only separate from God, but subordinate to him.[102]

As seen in the previous section, the influence of Hellenism upon Judaism was limited. It stopped short of any theological shift toward a blurring of God and man. As Holladay's exhaustive study of the writings of Philo and Josephus shows, the gap pictured between God and man actually widened. This may be due to the reaction of knowledgeable Jews. Aware of the beliefs in Hellenism with regard to the natures of God and man, writers such as Philo may be seen to bend Old Testament figures such as Moses in the direction of the Hellenistic wise man. Yet he cannot be faulted for confusing the natures of God and man. As a summary to his examination of Philo, Holladay offers a lengthy quote from C. H. Dodd with which the former agrees. The quote reads in part,

> True to his Jewish upbringing, Philo keeps the distinction between God and man. . . . For Philo God is eternally other than man. . . . Philo is here in harmony with the whole biblical tradition, in both Testaments . . . Here we come at once upon the ambiguity of duality which runs through all Philo's thought. Up to a point he will use the language which is natural to the

---

who could act as mediator and redeemer was no longer needed. *The Son of God*, 24.

[98]W. D. Davies, 164.

[99]Eichrodt, 2:373.

[100]Von Rad, *Old Testament Theology*, 1:218.

[101]Oscar Cullmann, *Christology of the New Testament*, trans. Shirley Guthrie and Charles Hall (Philadelphia: The Westminster Press, 1963), 272.

[102]James Robert Edwards, "The Son of God: Its Antecedents in Judaism and Hellenism and Its Use in the Earliest Gospel," (Ph.D. dissertation, Fuller Theological Seminary, 1978), 131-32.

Hermetists, but it does not always mean exactly the same thing to him. On the one hand he shares the religious outlook of Greek thinkers from Plato, whose God was the metaphysical Absolute, the One beyond the many. On the other hand, he is deeply influenced by the piety of the Old Testament, which no amount of allegorical exegesis can wholly resolve into a mystical absorption into the One. Up to a point he is able to reconcile the two ways of religion, but in the end they remain unassimilated.[103]

Summary

This chapter has presented several criticisms of the divine man Christology. Carelessness in the use of literary sources is evident when this approach refers to writings concerning miracle-working divine men which must be dated after the appearing of the New Testament writings. Even Philostratus' *Life of Apollonius of Tyana*, considered one of the best examples of the portrayal of the divine man,[104] cannot be dated before the third century A.D.[105] Philostratus claims to rely upon the memoirs of Apollonius handed on by one named Damis. But such memoirs are held to be a fraud.[106]

The divine man Christology is in no better position to cite the use of the term *theios anēr* in pre-Christian times. Even advocates of this position realize there is no specific application of the term. It could be employed to refer not only to miracle-workers, but also prophets, philosophers, exorcists, gifted orators, etc.[107] Holladay's criticism of the divine man Christology is the most damaging at this point. He says,

> Our fundamental criticism of the use of the expression *theios anēr* in Christological discussions arises from its intrinsic ambiguity. Long before this study, several scholars had already begun to express doubts about the legitimacy and propriety of using *theios anēr* as a *terminus technicus* or as a concrete, well-defined category, but this study has tended to reinforce those

---

[103]C. H. Dodd, *The Interpretation of the Fourth Gospel,* 60-61, quoted in Holladay, 197-98.

[104]Moses Hadas, *Heroes and Gods* (New York: Harper & Row, 1965), 7.

[105]Kee, *Community of the New Age,* 17.

[106]John Ferguson, *The Religions of the Roman Empire* (Ithaca, NY: Cornell University Press, 1970), 182.

[107]Helmut Koester, "The Structure and Criteria of Early Christian Beliefs," in *Trajectories through Early Christianity* (Philadelphia: Fortress Press, 1971), 216-17.

doubts. The obvious again needs pointing out: the single word
theios was capable of *at least* four distinct meanings, with room
for intermediate shades and this fluidity has been attested with
the Hellenistic-Jewish authors, specifically Josephus and Philo.
Thus, because *theios anēr* is automatically capable of *at least*
four meanings, including "divine man," "inspired man," "a
man, in some sense, related to God," and "extraordinary man,"
it is less possible to speak without further ado of *a* [specific]
theios anēr Christology, as if *theios anēr* had only one meaning,
especially as if the two notions of divinity and miracle-working
were essential ingredients. Unlike the υἱός θεοῦ in which the
Father-son model remains constant, even though the expression
itself may be taken metaphorically or literally, *theios anēr* has
no such built-in control.[108]

With such ambiguity within the use of the term, one wonders
how it can be viewed as a meaningful background to New Testament
Christology. The more narrow application with reference to miracle-
working was seen to have occurred only in the post-Christian era.

The divine man approach most generally accepts the assumption
that the concept came to be applied to Christ through its use by
Hellenistic Jews. Using Philo and Josephus as prime examples,
divine man advocates claim the use of the term by these men
demonstrates their assimilation of the Hellenistic concept of God and
man into their thinking. As Holladay points out, this represents an
uncritical and careless reading of these men. To have seen Philo's
and Josephus' writings thusly would have been "appalling" to
them.[109] Rather, their writings maintain the strict dichotomy between the natures of God and man characteristic to orthodox Jewry.

The absence of a critical differentiation between the Hellenistic
and biblical thought-worlds is seen in the divine man approach. A.
D. Nock makes a good point when he says,

> The existence of the θεῖος ἄνθρωπος in Syria and in the Hellenistic
> world perhaps made it easier for converts to grasp the idea of a
> more than human teacher having lived in the world, and passed
> from it to take definitely divine rank. [But] It does not explain the
> recognition of Jesus as Son of God, and as Lord by the com-
> munity at Jerusalem.[110]

108Holladay, 237.
109Ibid., 197.
110A. D. Nock, 1:86.

That is, even if it could be conceded that the term *theios anēr* was a fixed concept in the Hellenistic world, it would not explain why Palestinian Jews continued to view him as the Son of God. This is the subject of the next chapter. As the final chapter it will specifically critique the view that the concept of the divine man stands behind the Christological title "Son of God."

5

The "Divine Man" as Explanation for the New Testament "Son of God"

The previous chapter showed the inconsistencies in the position which sees the Hellenistic divine man as a background to the New Testament portrayal of Christ. This chapter will critique the assertion that this concept lay behind the title "Son of God" as applied to Jesus. The method for this critique will be to demonstrate the incongruity between the two titles by comparing the differing applications and cultural backgrounds of the titles. The first area of examination will be the use of the term θεῖος in the New Testament.

The New Testament Use of the Term θεῖος

The New Testament nowhere uses the designation θεῖος ἀνήρ/ἄνθρωπος. As Tiede shows, this is not an insignificant point to note.[1] So much has been made of the concept and its influence on the New Testament portrayal of Christ, that its absence is disquieting.

But the term θεῖος (or a derivative) does appear in three New Testament passages. In Acts 17:29 we read, "Being the offspring of God, we should not think that the divine nature [θεῖον] is like gold or silver or stone . . ." Paul says in Rom. 1:20, "his invisible attributes, his eternal power and divine nature [θειότης] . . . The reference in 2 Peter 1:3-4 reads, "his divine [θείας] power has granted to us everything pertaining to life and godliness. . . . For by these he has granted to us his precious and magnificent promises, so that by them you may become sharers of the divine nature [θείας] . . ." (1:3, 4). A brief examination of these uses is necessary.

The first usage, that of Acts 17:29, is in the discourse Paul delivers on Mars Hill. This is not typical Pauline language. Hanson says this "is an unusual way of referring to God, conveying a rather remote and impersonal impression."[2] Why then would Paul employ

---

[1]David Lenz Tiede, *The Charismatic Figure as Miracle Worker* (Missoula, MT: Scholars Press, 1972), 254, n. 33.

[2]R. P. C. Hanson, *The Acts* (Oxford: Clarendon Press,1967), 182.

such terminology? Moulton and Milligan point out that papyri evidence shows frequent use of this term, and therefore demonstrates that in the context of Acts 17, "Paul, in addressing an audience of heathen philosophers, adapts his language to them."[3]

Paul refers to the divine nature of God when he employs θειότης in Rom. 1:20. In this context Paul is speaking of the attributes of God which are visible and have been seen clearly by mankind in history. Cranfield says of the word, "It is a Hellenistic term . . . denoting the divine nature and properties; and is to be distinguished from θεότης ('deity'), which denotes the divine personality."[4] Charles Hodge says the term θειότης denotes "divine excellence in general . . . [whereas] θεότης on the other hand expresses the being rather than the excellence of God. The latter is Godhead, the former is divinity . . ."[5]

The final use of the term in 2 Peter would appear to be somewhat more problematic. Here Peter speaks of the "granting of" and the "sharing of" the divine nature (θείας). Unlike the previous two references which employed the term exclusively with reference to God, Peter uses the term to speak of a benefit granted to the believer by God. Michael Green offers an apt explanation of Peter's usage of the term,

> This certainly looks startling, but the form of the expression has now been paralleled by the Decree of Stratonicea to the honour of Zeus and Hecate. Further, contemporaries such as Philo, Strobaeus and Josephus use similar language, which shows that this sort of talk was current coin in the first century A.D., and as such Peter could have used it for his purpose as readily as the modern preacher talks of the quantum theory without in the least necessarily understanding all its implications. But is the idea, of being partaker of the divine nature, too advanced for Peter? It is intrinsically no different from being born from above (Jn. 3:3; Jas. 1:18; 1 Pet. 1:23), being the temple of the Holy Spirit (1 Cor. 6:19), being in Christ (Rom. 8:1) or being the dwelling-place of the Trinity (Jn. 14:17-23). In this whole introductory paragraph of his Epistle, the writer is putting his Christian doctrine into Greek dress for the purposes of communication, without in the least committing himself to the pagan associations of

---

[3]James Hope Moulton and George Milligan, *The Vocabulary of the Greek Testament*, reprint ed. (Grand Rapids: Wm.B. Eerdmans Publishing Company, 1982), 285.

[4]C. E. B. Cranfield, *A Critical and Exegetical Commentary on the Epistle to the Romans* (Edinburgh: T. & T. Clark, 1975), 1:115.

[5]Charles Hodge, *A Commentary on Romans* (Carlisle, PA: Banner of Truth Trust, 1975), 55.

the terms.[6]

The New Testament, therefore, employs the term θεῖος and derivatives as a diminutive or adjectival form of the term θεός.[7] It is only by relation with God (θεός) that the term comes into association with man.[8] That is, the term is used only to speak of the manifestation of God's nature and is only applied to man as that which God grants to those who believe in Jesus Christ. This is not to say, of course, that man becomes God or that God is lessened in his nature. Nothing of God's essential nature (θεός) is given to the regenerated man. The θεῖος granted to a believing individual is that aspect of God's nature which he chooses to share. As Kleinknecht says, employing the term θεῖος implies no surrender of personal faith in God by New Testament writers.[9] There is no co-mingling of the natures of God and man.

Even more importantly for the present discussion, however, is the point Goppelt makes: "θεῖος" is not used once with reference to Jesus Christ.[10] If the concept of the *theios anēr* does indeed stand behind the New Testament portrayal of Jesus and his title "Son of God," one should certainly expect *some* reference to him in this regard. Yet, the New Testament never employs the term in this way.

The New Testament evidences a different application of the cognates of the term θεῖος than do secular Greek writings, therefore. Whereas the term θεῖος was employed by Greeks to speak of man's sharing of God's very nature, the New Testament differentiates between that which is exclusively God's (θεός) and that which he chooses to share (θεῖος) with those who believe.

There are other differentiations to be seen. Specifically with regard to the titles "Son of God" and *theios anēr*, there is much diversity to be noted. The next section will examine this diversity.

The Lack of Congruity between the Two Titles

This section is devoted to pointing up the irreconcilable differences

---

[6]Michael Green, *The Second Epistle of Peter and the General Epistle of Jude* (Grand Rapids: Wm. B. Eerdmans Publishing Company, 1979), 24-25.

[7]*Theological Dictionary of the New Testament*, s.v. "θεός," by Hermann Kleinknecht, 3 (1965):122.

[8]Ibid.

[9]Ibid.

[10]Leonard Goppelt, *Theology of the New Testament*, trans. John E. Alsup (Grand Rapids: Wm. B. Eerdmans, 1982) 2:71.

that exist between the two titles. The first of these differences to be considered is that of cultural backgrounds.

The diverse cultural backgrounds of the titles

Even Bultmann conceded that there was no "divine man" present in the Old Testament.[11] But Bultmann emphasized the Hellenistic influence upon the gospel accounts almost to the exclusion of Old Testament traditions.[12] Bultmann's opinion that the gospel accounts were more in the Hellenistic than the Old Testament vein may stem from the observation that Greek culture ascribed divinity quite readily to great men whereas Judaism did not.[13]

Yet it is interesting to note that even those Jewish writers who have been viewed as "Hellenistic" are reluctant to apply the term "son of God" to men. Philo is quite restrained in his use of the term, applying it only to angels and not outstanding men in salvation history. For these men he employs the Old Testament term "men of God."[14]

Even if the Gospels are considered to be greatly influenced by Hellenism, there would still be difficulty in the use of the title "Son of God." Edwards points out that, although Greek thought saw all men as "sons of God" to some extent, yet the title is not so common in Hellenism.[15] This title, therefore, cannot be substituted synonymously for the concept of "divine man."[16] Von Martitz points out that the assumption made by Wetter and those who followed him that "son of God" was a title of the divine man cannot be verified from Greek texts.[17]

Concerning the Son of God title, I. H. Marshall says, "In view of the undoubted Palestinian Jewish character of many of its occurrences, the possibility of Hellenistic derivation can be once and for all ruled out . . . It is more common to understand the title in terms of messiahship."[18] On this subject Longenecker says,

---

[11]Rudolf Bultmann, *Primitive Christianity in Its Contemporary Setting*, trans. Reginald H. Fuller (New York: Meridian Books, 1957), 48.

[12]Tiede, 248.

[13]Martin Hengel, *The Son of God*, trans. John Bowden (Philadelphia: Fortress Press, 1976), 38.

[14]Ibid., 53-55.

[15]James Robert Edwards, "The Son of God: Its Antecedents in Judaism and Hellenism and Its Use in the Earliest Gospel" (Ph.D. dissertation, Fuller Theological Seminary, 1978), 79.

[16]Ibid.

[17]*Theological Dictionary of the New Testament*, s.v. "υἱός," by Wülfing von Martitz, 8 (1972):338-39.

[18]I. Howard Marshall, "Son of God or Servant of Yahweh?--A Reconsideration

"Son of God" was no alien import, and certainly cannot be interpreted simply in terms of popular religious notions circulating in the Hellenistic world. Contrary to the assumption of a Hellenistic provenance, it is in the literature of the Jewish mission of the church that the ascriptions "Son of God" and "Son" come most to expression, and not, it must be noted, in that representing the Gentile cycle of witness. It is Matthew among the Synoptics who gives increased prominence to the sonship of Jesus, John who makes this theme the high point of his Christology, and Hebrews that devotes more than two chapters to its explication. In comparison Paul's employment of "son of God" only three times and "the Son" twelve seems rather surprising.[19]

The more infrequent use of the title by Paul--the apostle to the Gentiles--would seem alarming in light of its occurrence in other New Testament books. This does not mean, however, that Paul's perspective of the title is different from those other writers. Brandon Byrne says,

> There is, then,"no need to go beyond Judaism to account for Paul's "sonship of God" idea . . . with respect to his understanding of Christ as Son of God. What is indeed remarkable is the considerable affinity of Paul's "sonship of God" theology with that of a work so early and so thoroughly "Palestinian" as *Jubilies* . . . the charge of eclecticism [that Paul drew from Palestinian tradition here, Hellenistic there] can be countered by pointing to the fact that precisely this [Byrne's] study of sonship and associated themes has shown . . . [that] behind the faith of the early Christian community in which Paul's own faith was nurtured lay a Jewish milieu the conceptual complexity and resourcefulness of which becomes even more apparent.[20]

The struggle which many scholars had in seeing the "Son of God" title in the New Testament as non-Jewish stemmed from the difficulty in viewing the writings as essentially Jewish in nature. This was especially true of John's writings. On this Smith says,

---

of Mark I.11." *New Testament Studies* 15 (1968/69):335.

[19]Richard N. Longenecker, *The Christology of Early Jewish Christianity* (Naperville, IL: Alec R. Allenson, Inc., 1972), 98.

[20]Brendon Byrne, *"Sons of God--Seed of Abraham"* (Rome: Biblical Institute Press, 1979), 220-21.

Earlier quests for the religious background of the Johannine literature have ranged the field from Hellenistic philosophy, to Mystery religions, even to Buddhism, and more recently to Mandaeism and Gnosticism. . . . In recent years, however, Jewish circles interacting with Johannine Christianity have been increasingly regarded as the proximate background and seedbed of the Fourth Gospel. This has come about . . . as a result of a recognition of the number of distinctively Jewish features in the Fourth Gospel . . .[21]

Concerning the Gospel of John, Fennema adds,

John's view of Jesus' relationship to God, for example, is thoroughly grounded in traditional Jewish imagery. . . . In short, by emphasizing concepts which are distinctively their own, John invites the Jews to accept Jesus as a heavenly being, who functions as God himself.[22]

Perhaps even more difficult for some scholars to see as distinctively Jewish and not Hellenistic, is the frequency of miraculous deeds by Jesus. These, they would argue, certainly betray Hellenistic influence upon the Gospel writers.

But there is counter-argument that the miraculous deeds of Jesus represent a continuation of Old Testament tradition. Kee says that, "miraculous deeds of specially-endowed men did not originate in the Hellenistic period, nor was interest in these . . . indigenous to Greece or to Hellenistic culture. . . . [it is] well represented in the Old Testament canon itself . . ."[23] Concerning the Marcan portrayal of Jesus, Otto Betz says,

Was the Son of God in Mark, with the miracles which he performed, depicted essentially along Hellenistic lines? I doubt it . . . Bultmann has overestimated Hellenistic influence . . . even if such a [divine man] type did exist, the New Testament scholar should be much more inclined to look back to the "men of God" of the Old Testament. . . . We need not dispute that the Jesus of the miracle stories accorded with the hope of Hellen-

---

[21]Dwight Moody Smith, Jr. *John* (Philadelphia: Fortress Press, 1976), 9-10.

[22]David Allen Fennema, "Jesus and God According to John: An Analysis of the Fourth Gospel's Father/Son Christology" (Ph.D. dissertation, Duke University, 1979), 261.

[23]Howard Kee, *Community of the New Age* (Philadelphia: The Westminster Press, 1977), 24.

istic man, though he plays no part in Paul, the apostle to the Gentiles. . . . we must look at the Marcan miracles in the light of the Old Testament tradition and Jewish exegesis, and then decide what is left for Hellenism and its "divine man."[24]

With specific reference as to how the miracles of Jesus continue in the Old Testament tradition, Betz continues,

While [the miracle stories] present Jesus above all as the second Moses, the tradition of the young David and the prophets Elijah and Elisha have also had their various influences. When the men of Qumran wanted to strengthen faith they conjured up the memories of Moses and David: the annihilation of the Egyptians at the Red Sea and the victory over Goliath showed that God can bring about great things through his chosen ones. . . .There was a rabbinic belief that the second deliverer, the Messiah, would be like the first, Moses, and the Christians, too saw a prefigurement of Jesus in the miracles done by Moses (Acts 7:36-7).

According to Mark, the power by which Jesus did his miracles is that of the Holy Spirit, which he had received at his baptism (Mark 1:9-11). David, too, had once been anointed with the Spirit of God before he emerged as Israel's helper: he was the man after God's heart (1 Sam. 13:14; Acts 13:22) and received the Spirit as a permanent possession (1 Sam. 16:13). The same thing is meant when, according to the account of the baptism of Jesus, the Holy Spirit descends upon Jesus like a dove . . .[25]

Jesus' working of miracles included the act of exorcism. This concept presents a problem for the divine man approach because,

Exorcisms were uncommon among Hellenistic "divine men." Although healings or resuscitations are frequently found in Hellenistic literature, seldom do we encounter a "divine man" expelling a demon. . . . On the other hand, "unclean spirits" (Mk. 1:23; 3:11; 5:2) and "God Most High" (5:7) appear as common places in Jewish literature.[26]

Moreover, Kee points out that the verb to "command" ($\dot{\epsilon}\pi\iota\tau\iota\mu\dot{\alpha}\omega$), e.g.

---

[24]Otto Betz, *What Do We Know about Jesus?* (Philadelphia: The Westminster Press, 1968), 64-67.
[25]Ibid., 67-68.
[26]Edwards, 129.

Mk. 1:25; 3:12; 4:39; 9:25) is never used with reference to exorcisms in Hellenistic literature, but rather is found as a *terminus technicus* in exorcisms described in Jewish literature, including Qumran.[27]

The miracles of Jesus, rather than manifesting a Hellenistic influence, point to the influence of Messianism. Ulrich Mauser says,

> The great influence of the wilderness motif on the Messianic ideology is seen in its political implications in several passages in Josephus. Since the Messiah was believed to arise in the wilderness and gather the people there, the Judean desert was repeatedly the scene where Messianic movements were gathering, although the various movements apparently had different political colours.[28]

With specific relation to Jesus, Mauser writes, "An appreciation of the wilderness ideology behind the narrative of Jesus' miracles would counter the facile assumption that such responses by the populaces stem from a θεῖος ἀνήρ perspective."[29] In Chapter 2 this study showed that the concept of "Son of David" was seen as a plausible explanation for the part which miracles played in Jesus' Messiahship. Dennis Duling says that this information about Jesus' miracleworkings as the "Son of David" could ultimately mean "a fallout in the 'divine man' discussions."[30]

Jesus' miracles served another purpose in the Old Testament tradition: they stood as a sign of who he was. Otto Betz explains,

> In general, the Old Testament and the milieu of Jewish exegesis help to explain best the miracles in the gospels. Moreover, they cannot have originated in . . . a Judaism free from eschatological expectations and apocalyptic ideas. For these miracles are signs pointing to the great revelation of righteousness in the near future; they are impressions of the apocalyptic mood. The interest in the manifestation of the power of Jesus, which is certainly characteristic for these miracles, was not kindled by the necessity of making him a successful competition of Hellenistic Divine Men. For these saving deeds were demanded by

---

[27]Howard C. Kee, "The Terminology of Mark's Exorcism Stories," *New Testament Studies* 14 (1968):232-46.

[28]Ulrich W. Mauser, *Christ in the Wilderness* (Naperville, IL: Alec R. Allenson, 1963), 57-58.

[29]Ibid., 56.

[30]Dennis C. Duling, "Solomon, Exorcism, and the Son of David," *Harvard Theological Review* 68 (1975):236.

Jewish messianism. The Christ had to be 'attested by God' with mighty works and wonders (Acts 2:22); the Jews asked for signs (1 Cor. 1:22). Moreover, the miracles of Jesus were not told primarily to overcome the disappointment because of the delayed Parousia. Their emphasis on the present does not do away with the future. They reveal the presence of the Messiah with whom the kingdom is beginning to be realized (Mt. 12:28).[31]

In another place the same author writes,

> In his healing of the blind, the deaf and the lame, Jesus fulfills the Old Testament expectation of the time of salvation (Isa. 35:3-6; 61:1-2). . . . Such miracles were "signs" of Israel's leader and deliverer sent by God.[32]

The Jews looked for a miraculous sign because this was a part of their tradition as it flowed from the Old Testament. Kee says, "In the biblical tradition . . . there is a rich tradition in which various persons are described as having been enabled by God to perform miracles in fulfillment of his purposes. In this tradition the characteristic and appropriate term for the miracles is 'sign' . . ."[33]

In summary, unlike the Hellenistic designation "divine man," Jews were reluctant to ascribe sonship to even the greatest of men. The term was inexorably associated with Jewish Messianism and flowed from Old Testament tradition. This tradition was also the background against which the miracles of Jesus must be seen.

The fact that Jesus performed miracles as a sign of his Messiahship and Sonship points to another matter for consideration. Let us proceed to contrast the diverse applications of the titles *theios anēr* and "Son of God."

The diverse application of the titles

For all of the efforts of the advocates of the divine man Christology, the insurmountable hurdle has been that of the great differences that exist between the application of the *theios anēr* title and that of "Son of God." Even in the Hellenistic culture there is no

---

[31]Otto Betz, "The Concept of the So-called 'Divine Man' in Mark's Christology," in *Studies in New Testament and Early Christian Literature*, ed. David E. Aune (Leiden: E. J. Brill, 1972), 239-40.

[32]Idem, *What Do We Know about Jesus?* 67-68.

[33]Howard C. Kee, *Community of the New Age*, 25.

apparent mixing of these two titles.[34] Moreover, Nock shows that the title "son of God" was not a designation in the Hellenistic world for a miracle worker.[35]

In the same context, Nock says concerning the divine man,

> The inspired man, θεῖος ἄνθρωπος, is an important figure in the religious life of the time. Yet it must be remembered . . . that in any case this terminology is the consequence of the impression made by personalities; it does not create belief. The Christian who called Jesus Son of God denoted something precise by the term.[36]

Nock goes on to say that even though a ruler or charismatic figure such as a divine man may have been deified in legend,[37] this deification was not taken seriously and the individual who was deified was never to become the object of true worship.[38] The case of Jesus is quite different.The diversities extend to more than just the irreconcilability of the terms θεῖος ἀνήρ and υἱός θεοῦ. Edwards says,

> Not only in nomenclature, but also in model, *theios anēr* is ill-suited to the New Testament. . . . Thus, to assume that a "divine man" figure provides a prototype for Markan Christology is insufficient. . . . Jesus shared little in common with the poet inspired by the Muses, or the flamboyant claims of the Caesars. . . . The heroic feats of a Hercules leave few points of contact with the humble carpenter of Nazareth.[39]

We saw in chapter 3 how the works of Jesus pointed to his person and thus did more than serve as a mere functional role. Edwards points out that,

> The Greeks customarily used the term *moira* . . . as a basis for apotheosis. The idea of *moira*, merit, renders the concept of "divine man" in a primarily functional sense, not ontological, often with little or no spiritual content.[40]

---

[34]von Martitz, "υἱός," 8:338-40.

[35]Arthur Darby Nock, *Essays on Religion and the Ancient World,*, ed. Zeph Stewart (Oxford: Clarendon Press, 1972), 1:85.

[36]Ibid., 85-86.

[37]Ibid., 250.

[38]Ibid., 151.

[39]Edwards, 128.

[40]Ibid., 73.

The term μοῖρα cannot be found to characterize Jesus' ministry. In the same way, Nicol shows that the words for miracle which are used in association with the *theios anēr* in Hellenism include θαῦμα and ἀρετή.[41] These terms are not employed by the Gospel writers.

Another incongruity between the Hellenistic divine man and the person of Jesus is that of preexistence. Hengel says,

> Of course, from the heroes of the iron age onwards, Greece is familiar with the physical descent of great warriors and wise men from individual gods, and stories of miraculous births are associated with them as in the case of Pythagoras, Plato, Alexander, Augustus and Apollonius of Tyana. However, we do not find in this context the combination of pre-existence and sending into the world which is typical of Pauline Christology.[42]

Nock adds, ". . . the θεῖοι ἄνθρωποι of historical times are hardly ever credited with an earlier personal form of existence, except by way of metempsychosis . . ."[43]

One of the major differences which exists between Jesus and the Hellenistic divine man is that of Jesus' suffering and death. Dunn says, "If there is anything that can properly be called a 'divine man' Christology . . . which can be said to have influenced the presentation of Jesus as a miracle worker . . . then the point to note is that [Paul and the evangelists] provide a sharp corrective by emphasizing that the character of the gospel is determined by the suffering and death of Jesus."[44]

Now this is not to say that there was no mention of suffering for any of the divine men in Hellenistic literature. Tiede shows that besides performing miracles, suffering and even death were sometimes viewed as an authentication of divine status.[45] But as Fortna points out, "These two criteria for identifying divine men--miracles and suffering--are usually quite distinct, and often in competition with each other . . . But . . . the death of Jesus is as much his own act as God's, and thus calls attention to him in much the same way the signs do; and in the end it is the necessary prelude to the greatest of

---

[41]W. Nicol, *The Sēmeia in the Fourth Gospel* (Leiden: E. J. Brill, 1972), 63.

[42]Hengel, 31.

[43]Nock, 2:934-35.

[44]James D. G. Dunn, "Demythologyzing--The Problem of Myth in the New Testament," in *New Testament Interpretation*, ed. I. Howard Marshall (Grand Rapids: Wm. B. Eerdmans, 1977), 293.

[45]Tiede, 59.

his signs, his own resurrection."[46] This contrast between miracle-working and suffering is addressed by Edwards with relation to the crucifixion narrative in Mark,

> Here the *theios anēr* argument meets an insurmountable obstacle. If the centurion were familiar with the gods and "divine men" of the Greco-Roman culture, it would be out of his frame of reference, indeed in direct contradiction to it, to call Jesus a son of God at this point of degradation and death. . . . a confession evoked by an earthly triumph would have been expected; a confession in the wake of the crucifixion scarcely squares with a Hellenistic background.[47]

Perhaps the greatest inconsistency in the divine man picture which presents a glaring problem for the divine man Christology is the issue of miracle-working. This is viewed by the divine man advocates as the most common feature of the *theios anēr*.[48] Yet this is the very point at which Jesus is different from divine men. Bornkamm et. al. say that the account of the temptation of Jesus and his refusal to perform miracles takes issue with what was obviously a widespread misunderstanding of Jesus as a Hellenistic miracle-worker. The gospel account, says Bornkamm, clearly moves away increasingly from the idea of the *theios anēr*.[49] On this same subject Fuller writes,

> Not only is the derivation palpably different from what Bultmann suggests; the meaning of "Son of God" in the Temptation narrative is wholly incompatible with its supposed derivation from Hellenistic sources. For the θεῖος ἀνήρ was preeminently one who called attention to his supernatural character by his wonderful deeds, whereas by quoting from Deuteronomy Jesus rejects precisely this as a diabolical temptation. Clearly then we have every right to look for a different origin and background to the application by the synoptic gospels of the title 'Son of God' to Jesus during his earthly life.[50]

---

[46]Robert Fortna, "Christology in the Fourth Gospel:Redaction-Critical Perspectives," *New Testament Studies* 21 (1975):91-92.

[47]Edwards, 183.

[48]Hans Dieter Betz, "Jesus as Divine Man," in *Jesus and the Historian*, ed. F. Thomas Trotter (Philadelphia: The Westminster Press, 1968), 116.

[49]Bornkamm, Gerhard Barth and Heinz Joachim Held, *Tradition and Interpretation in Matthew*, trans. Percy Scott (London: SCM Press, Ltd., 1963), 33-34.

[50]Reginald H. Fuller, *The Mission and Achievement of Jesus* (London: SCM

Concerning miracle-working in the ancient world, Edwards points out, "Miracle-workers of antiquity tended toward ostentation to substantiate their claims of supernatural endowment . . . [but] Jesus expressly forbade those whom he healed to say a word about him and he refused to provide signs as proof of who he was (Mk. 8:11-13)."[51] Of Jesus' healing the paralytic in Mark 2:1-2 Edwards comments, "Aside from the fact that no Hellenistic miracle-worker claimed authority to forgive sins, the story reveals again that Jesus performed signs and wonders of healing not 'to make a display' but as a sign of the in-breaking of God's reign on earth."[52] Indeed, as Cullmann points out, when Jesus' miracles are studied, they show not only "miraculous power, but the absolute obedience of a Son in the execution of divine commission."[53]

The portrayal of Jesus was thus very different from that of the Hellenistic divine man. Jesus' miracles were not merely a "show," but a manifestation of a most unique individual. Fortna says,

> One of the characteristics of the aretalogy, the usual vehicle for displaying divine men and distinguishing among them, is a cataloguing of divine titles applicable to the hero in question. Yet each of the titles employed by . . . John points not to a thaumaturge, one among others, but to an utterly unique figure: lamb of God, the one of whom Moses and the prophets wrote, the Prophet, king of Israel . . . Messiah.[54]

These differences--the dichotomy in the Hellenistic world between the titles υἱός θεοῦ and θεῖος ἀνήρ, the absence of Hellenistic terms to characterize Jesus' life, which were often used to refer to the θεῖος ἀνήρ, the major role Jesus' suffering and death played in the portrayal of his life, and the contrast between Jesus' miracle-working and that of the Hellenistic divine men--would seem to make the figure of the Hellenistic divine man incongruous with the gospel portrait of Jesus. Had the gospel writers intended to present a figure more in keeping with what the divine man advocates see as the archtypical divine man, certainly they could have made their accounts correspond better to that figure. That there is little correspon-

---

Press, 1954), 81-82.

[51]Edwards, 129-30.

[52]Ibid., 130.

[53]Oscar Cullmann, *Christology of the New Testament*, trans. Shirley Guthrie and Charles Hall (Philadelphia: The Westminster Press, 1963), 276.

[54]Fortna, 493-94.

dence seems to lend evidence that this is not the case.

CONCLUSION

The purpose of this study has been to evaluate the divine man Christology to determine if it stands as an adequate and objective background to the New Testament portrayal of Jesus. The conclusion would appear to be that this approach is neither adequate nor objective.

The divine man approach begins with the assumption that Jesus is to be viewed "making use of motifs from the Hellenistic concept of the Divine Man."[1] Inherent in this approach, however, is what Otto Betz terms ". . . the danger of a methodological circle: New Testament passages are used for building up a concept that is claimed to be the foundation of these passages."[2] He continues in the same reference to say, "I cannot understand why in this case we should be in need of a Hellenistic concept when the Old Testament . . . and the milieu of Jewish exegesis help to explain best the miracles in the gospels."[3] On this topic Hengel adds,

> The Jewish Christians were always the spiritual driving force which determined the content of theology. In fact they put their stamp on the whole of the first-century church. Unfortunately the history of religions school paid too little attention to this decisive point. The men who carried on the spiritual controversy with Judaism most sharply during the first century A.D. come from Judaism . . .[4]

Goppelt addresses this point saying,

> Hellenistic Christians did not think about divine sonship any longer in terms of Hellenistic concepts about deity but in terms of

---

[1]Hans Dieter Betz, "Jesus as Divine Man," in *Jesus and the Historian*, ed. F. Thomas Trotter (Philadelphia: The Westminster Press, 1968), 116.

[2]Otto Betz, "The Concept of the So-Called 'Divine Man' in Mark's Christology," in *Studies in New Testament and Early Christian Literature*, ed. David Edward Aune (Leiden: E. J. Brill, 1972), 232.

[3]Ibid.

[4]Martin Hengel, *The Son of God*, trans. John Bowden (Philadelphia: Fortress Press, 1976), 67.

the God of the Old Testament. They had turned away from the
former and come to the latter; that was the central content of
their conversion (1 Thess. 1:9). . . . Even for Hellenistic
Christians the title "Son of God" placed Jesus in a special relationship to the God of the Old Testament. He was not the depth of
the cosmos but the personal One standing in relationship to all
that existed in the world.[5]

Because of this, Goppelt sees Bultmann's transference theory as "an
oversimplification."[6]

This is not to say, however, that the employing of the title "Son of
God" was not based on some existing conception of *that* title. As Cullmann points out, "We must avoid being so fearful of falling into an
uncritical conservatism that we rule out entirely *a priori* the possibility that the first Christians--and perhaps even Jesus himself--
could have filled an old expression with a completely new content."[7]
Thus the "Son of God" came to mean *more* than anticipated from the
Old Testament but something fundamentally *different* from that in
the Hellenistic world.

But this same argument for the *theios anēr* as background to the
portrayal of Christ is problematical. Nock suggests that, "The existence of the θεῖος ἄνθρωπος in Syria and in the Hellenistic world perhaps made it easier for converts to grasp the idea of a more than human teacher having lived in the world."[8] But as chapter 4 showed, too
many different applications and basic anachronisms exist to permit
an acceptance of this title as a fixed concept at or before the time of
Jesus Christ.[9] It seems more reasonable, as LaGrange suggests, to
see the Hellenistic hero as miracle-worker to exist because of the
influence of the Gospels rather than vice-versa.[10]

But even if some accounts of wonder-working were prevalent in
the first-century A.D., there is still good reason to accept the gospel
record. Achtemeier offers a thought-provoking argument on this
point,

---

[5]Leonhard Goppelt, *Theology of the New Testament*, trans. John Alsup (Grand
Rapids: William B. Eerdmans, 1982), 2:71.

[6]Ibid.

[7]Oscar Cullmann, *The Christology of the New Testament*, trans. Shirley
Guthrie and Charles Hall (Philadelphia: The Westminster Press, 1963), 270-71.

[8]Arthur Darby Nock, *Essays on Religion and the Ancient World*, ed. Zeph
Stewart (Oxford: Clarendon Press, 1972), 1:86.

[9]See above, pp. 99-106.

[10]R.P.M. LaGrange, "Les Legendes Pythagoriennes et L'Evangile," *Revue
Biblique* 46 (1936/37):510-11, 27.

If, then, the primitive church were [sic] going to hand on the traditions about the mighty acts of Jesus, they ran the risk of telling accounts that at best were ambiguous, at worst capable of making Jesus appear to be just another of those wandering magicians so familiar to the Hellenistic world. Given those circumstances, the fact that such stories were preserved at all is perhaps the most persuasive evidence that Jesus did in fact do such things.[11]

As Sabourin says of these miracles, "The personality of Jesus remains in every case the decisive factor."[12] Concerning the person of Jesus portrayed in the Gospels, Davis adds, ". . . Jesus is as unique as the God of the Bible, and this uniqueness is crucial . . ."[13]

Perhaps the most important questions which the present writer could pose are: If Jesus is to be viewed as just another divine man, can it account for the large following of Palestinian Jews? Can this account for His immediate and devoted followers in contrast with the following of Hellenistic divine men which usually did not occur until generations later? Could that following have continued to exist in the face of unparalleled persecution?

Only the utter uniqueness of the person of Jesus Christ can account for the historical record of the Christian faith. Only the coming of God in human flesh can justify the portrayal of the one whom the New Testament calls "the Son of God."

---

[11]Paul J. Achtemeier, *Mark*. (Philadelphia: Fortress Press, 1975), 73.

[12]Leopold Sabourin, "Hellenistic and Rabbinic 'Miracles,'" *Biblical Theology Bulletin* 2 (1972):306.

[13]Philip George Davis, "'Truly this Man Was the Son of God': The Christological Focus of the Markan Redaction," (Ph.D. dissertation, McMaster University, 1979), p. 169.

Appendix

Page 12

[34]"Wer die antiken Vorstellungen näher kennt, wird finden, dass diese Gedanken allgemein mit dem θεῖος ἀνθρωπος in Verbindung gebracht werden. Die Fähigkeit, die Gedanken der Menschen zu erkennen, dessen auch später die christlichen Pneumatiker (vgl. z.B. Paulus im 1 Kor. 14, 24. 25 oder Ignatius, ad Trall. 5, 2), und in späterer Zeit auch Mönche ganz wie die wandernden Bettelpropheten des Hellenismus, sich rühmten, ist ein Zug, der so zu sagen selbstverständlich mit diesen Männern zusammengehören muss. Die Begnadigung, z. B. im voraus Tag und Stunde seines Todes zu wissen, wurde als einer der träfigsten Beweise dafür angesehen, dass der Mensch mit Gott in Verbindung stehe, dass er freien Zutritt (παρρησία) zu den geheimen Ratschlüssen des Vaters habe, also ganz göttlich, θεῖος sei. Eben daher ist wohl gerade der Zug von der Allwissenheit Jesu so oft im Evangelium hervorgehoben (vgl. 6, 6. 64. 70; 7, 19; 8, 21; 11, 4. 9. 11. 15; 13, 1ff. 18; 16, 19; 18, 4. 32 usw.)." Gillis P. Wetter, *Der Sohn Gottes* (Göttingen: Vandenhoeck & Ruprecht, 1916), 71-72.

Pages 12-13

[35]"Bis jetzt wir allgemeinere Züge in der Sohn Gottes-Gestalt der volkstümlichen hellenistischen Frömmigkeit festgestellt und gefunden, dass sie in den θεῖος ἀνθρωπος übergeht, ja mit ihm in mancher Hinsicht identisch zu sein scheint. Wir haben gesehen, wie ein Ausgangspunkt für die Vorstellung ein geschichtlicher ist: aus den gewaltigen grossen Taten, aus Geistesreden oder ähnl. gewisser Menschen hat man geschlossen, dass sie θεῖος, mit göttlichen Kräften ausgerüftet sind; ihre Weisheit, ihre höheren Kenntnisse zeugen dafür, dass sie 'Götter' sind." Ibid., 82-83.

Page 14

[41]"Und doch, die Frage brennt uns allem im Herzen: Wie steht das Christusbild zu der antiken Welt? Was ist etwa antikes Erbe darin, was spontane Parallelerscheinung? Was Wahrheit, was Legende? Fragen, leichter gestellt als beantwortet." Otto Weinreich, "Antikes Gottmenschentum," *Neues Jahrbücher für Wissenschaft und Jugenbildung* 2 (1926):650.

[47]" . . . wuchsen mir neue Erkenntnisse zu, vor allem öffneten sich mir in dieser Zeit ganz neue Aspekte: (1) die Gleichartigkeit der beiden Gestalten selbst, die Apostelhaftigkeit Jesu und die Christusähnlichkeit des Paulus, und (2) die Vergleichbarkeit beider Gestalten mit dem 'Gottesman' des A.T.'s und dem theios anthropos [no italics] der griechisch-römischen Antike." Hans Windisch, *Paulus und Christus* (Leipzig: J. C. Hinrichs'sche Buchhandlung, 1934), v.

Page 15
49"Das Stadium seiner Legende ist für das Verständnis Jesu und der Geschichte seiner Tradition nicht ohne Bedeutung und von theologischer Seite wohl
noch zu wenig betrieben. . . . Ja, man kann sogar sagen: die Jesusüberlieferung
steht nach Form und Gehalt der Pythagoraslegende ehreblich näher als der Geschichte oder Legende eines 'jüdischen Messias.'" Ibid., 59-60.

Page 16
57"Es sollte eine wesentliche Aufgabe dieser Arbeit sein, zu zeigen, dass die
Antike, zumal die spätere, und das frühe Christentum das gleiche Bild des göttlichen Menschen kennen." Ludwig Bieler, ΘΕΙΟΣ ANHP. Das Bild des "Göttlichen
Menschen" in Spätantike und Frühchristentum. (Wien: Buchhandlung Oskar Hö-
fels, 1935-36, 2 vols. Reprint Darmstadt: Wissenschaftliche Buchgesellschaft,
1976), 1:145.

59"Sie will vielmehr den Gesamttypus, gewissermassen die platonische Idee
des antiken Gottmenschen schauen lassen, der sich mag der einzelne θεῖος gleich
nie und nirgends alle wesenlichen Züge in letzter Vollkommenheit lückenlos in
sich vereinigen doch in jedem seiner Vertreter bald mehr, bald weniger ausprägt
. . ." Ibid., 1:4.

Page 17
62"Wo immer wir dem Worte θεῖος begegnen, sind wir im Kreise wo nicht des
Religiösen, doch sicher des 'Numinosen.'" Ibid.

Page 18
71"Zahlreich sind auch die Selbstaussagen von θεῖοι ἀνδρες durch die sie sich
für Gott oder Gottes Sohn erklären." Ibid., 1:137.

Pages 18-19
72"Und doch unterscheidet sich auch der Jesus des Johannesevangeliums sehr
wesentlich von jener υἱοί θεοῦ, den θεῖοι ἀνθρωπος des Hellenismus. . . . dass er
immer wieder hinter dem Vater zurücktritt . . . der sonst gerade die 'hellenistischen' Züge des johanneischen Christusbildes besonders unterstreicht." Ibid.,
1:138-39.

Page 19
75"Der θεῖος ἀνήρ ist zunächst--ganz allgemein gesagt--eine besondere Aus-
prägung des genialen Menschen, des Übermenschen oder wie immer man ihn
nennen mag, und zwar in der Richtung des religiösen Helden. Daraus folgt vor
allem eine stark und wesentliche Bindung an das Göttliche. Sein Lebenswerk ist
Dienst eines Gottes, Zeugnis für eine Gottheit, sein Wissen unmittelbar von Gott
gegeben, seine Lehre göttliche Offenbarung. Seine Wunder, mögen sie auch noch
so nahe Berührung mit dem Zauber haben, . . . sind nicht Magie . . . sondern
Theurgie und oft geradezu unmittelbarer Ausfluss göttlicher Kraft, die, nicht sel-

ten ganz konkret gedacht, durch den göttlichen Menschen nur hindurchgeht in ihm wie in einem Gefässe aufgespeichert ist: der θεῖος ἀνήρ ist Träger des Mana und geniesst als solcher schon im Leben religiöse Verehrung (vgl. Pfister II 616 ff.). Als Gesandter Gottes übt er seine Wundermacht nicht um ihrer selbst willen, wie so oft der Zauberer zu Spiel und Ergötzung des Volkes oder hoher Herren seine Kunst zum Besten gibt--Jesus vor Herodes ist ein bezeichnendes Beispiel dafür (Lc 23, 8)." Ibid., 1:141.

[76]"Oft ist der θεῖος ἀνήρ ein Mensch, den die Gottheit erwählt hat, öfter noch ist er von Gott gezeugt, manchmal selber Gott." Ibid., 1:142.

Pages 20-21

[83]"Das grosse Erlebnis für alle, die Jesus kannten, war gerade jene ungeheure Erhöhung, die sein Bild in ihrem Bewusstsein erfahren hatte: vom Rabbi Jesus, der gekreuzigt wurde, zum Kyrios Christos, der auferstanden ist; während sonst das jüdische wie das klassische Altertum zwischen dem göttlichen Menschen und der auf Erden wandelnden Gottheit streng scheidet, ist Christus eben beides: θεῖος ἀνήρ in den Augen seiner hellenistischen Zeitgenossen, θεός ἐπιφανής im Glauben seiner Bekenner." Ibid., 1:150.

Page 74

[71]"Hier ist, was Könige und Propheten hatten und erfehnten, erfüllt; hier ist ein Bussruf, 'mehr' als der des Propheten, und ein Wort der Freude, 'mehr' als das des ersten Davids-Sohnes. Hier ist der Messias Gottes, der König, und Prophet zugleich ist." Julius Schniewind, *Das Evangelium nach Matthäus*, reprint ed. (Göttingen: Vandenhoeck & Ruprecht, 1962), 163.

Index

Abba, 83, 91
Achtemeier, P., 30, 108, 111, 136
Alexander of Abonuteichus, 34
Apollonius of Tyana, 7, 9, 28, 29, 35, 36, 118, 119, 131
apotheosis, 8, 31, 112, 130
aretalogy, 28, 33, 111, 133
Aristotle, 17
Barr, J., 112
Barrett, C. K., 89
Bauckham, R., 82
Baur, F. C., 9, 35
Beasley-Murray, G. R., 75
Becker, J., 30
Berger, K., 72, 102
Betz, H. D., 25, 28, 29, 102, 104, 116
Betz, O., 11, 69, 73, 101, 105, 108, 112, 126, 127, 128, 135
Bieler, L., 9, 15, 16, 17, 18, 19, 20, 21, 25, 30, 32, 36, 99, 100, 101, 103, 113
Black, M., 65
Bornkamm, G., 132
Bousset, W., 8, 10, 11
Bretscher, P., 80
Bright, J., 56, 107
Bultmann, R., 1, 2, 9, 21, 22, 23, 24, 25, 26, 32, 33, 34, 38, 63, 86, 115, 116, 124, 136
Byrne, B., 43, 44, 50, 68, 79, 125
Cahn, Z., 108
Christology, 1, 2, 3, 5, 7, 9, 11, 13, 16, 22, 25, 27, 28, 29, 30, 31, 32, 33, 35, 36, 37, 39, 97, 99, 104, 108, 118, 119, 131, 132
Conzelmann, H., 30

Cooke, G., 43, 44, 50, 52, 53, 54, 59
Cranfield, C. E. B., 122
Cullmann, O., 81, 82, 91, 92, 117, 133, 136
Dahl, N. A., 65
Davey, J. E., 66
Davidic covenant, 54
Davies, W. D., 109, 114
Davis, P. G., 137
Delitzsch, F., 42, 55
Dibelius, M., 13, 24
divine kingship, 50, 51, 57, 59, 64
divine man, 1, 2, 3, 5, 7, 8, 9, 10, 11, 13, 14, 15, 16, 17, 18, 19, 20, 21, 22, 24, 25, 26, 27, 28, 29, 30, 31, 32, 33, 34, 35, 36, 37, 38, 39, 96, 97, 99, 100, 101, 102, 103, 104, 105, 106, 107, 108, 109, 111, 113, 114, 116, 117, 118, 119, 120, 121, 124, 126, 127, 128, 129, 130, 131, 132, 133, 134, 135, 137
Dodd, C. H., 117
Donahue, J. R., 66, 72
Driver, S. R., 47
Duling, D., 69, 128
Dunn, J. D. G., 65, 91, 94, 131
Edwards, J. R., 37, 54, 68, 78, 86, 89, 124, 130, 132, 133
Eichrodt, W., 45
Fennema, D., 87, 89, 90, 93, 126
Hahn, F., 25
Fischer, L., 72
Fitzmyer, J., 64, 88
Fohrer, G., 54, 56
Fortna, R. T., 70, 131, 133
Frankfort, H., 51, 56

Fuller, R. H., 10, 65, 77, 80, 81, 132
"General Pattern Theory," 51, 52
Georgi, D., 26, 27, 28, 34
Goldsmith, D., 69
Goppelt, L., 2, 24, 67, 87, 99, 135, 136
Green, M., 122
Gundry, R., 106
Haag, H., 54
Hadas, M., 28
Hahn, F., 25, 26, 27
Hanson, R. P. C., 121
Harrison, E. F., 68
Hellenism/Hellenistic concepts, 1, 2, 3, 7, 8, 9, 10, 11, 12, 13, 14, 16, 18, 19, 20, 21, 22, 23, 24, 25, 26, 27, 29, 30, 31, 35, 36, 37, 86, 97, 99, 102, 103, 104, 105, 106, 107, 108, 109, 110, 111, 112, 113, 114, 116, 117, 119, 120, 121, 122, 124, 125, 126, 127, 128, 129, 130, 131, 132, 133, 135, 136, 137, 140
Hellenistic Christianity, 24, 63
Hellenistic-Judaism, 7, 22, 34
Hengel, 40, 41, 89, 91, 108, 114, 116, 131, 135
history-of-religions, 1, 8, 14
Hodge, C., 122
Holladay, C., 103, 106, 109, 110, 113, 114, 115, 117, 118, 119
Homer, 9, 13, 17
Iamblichus, 100
van Iersel, B. M. F., 67, 68, 83
James, E. O., 52, 58
Jeremias, J., 45, 65, 70, 79, 83
Johnson, A. R., 53, 56
Josephus, 14, 21, 25, 72, 108, 109, 110, 114, 119, 122
Judaism, 10, 11, 14, 22, 26, 64, 65, 66, 77, 83, 84, 85, 91, 94, 106,

107, 108, 109, 110, 111, 112, 113, 114, 117, 125, 135
Kazmierski, C. R., 93
Käsemann, E., 27
Keck, L., 27, 28
Kee, H. C., 1, 65, 67, 70, 80, 102, 109, 111, 126, 127, 129
Kidding, K. A. H., 57
Kim, S., 66, 85
kingdom of God, 13, 35, 70, 71, 73, 75, 77, 129
Kingsbury, J. D., 27, 31, 37, 66, 67, 71, 75, 82, 91
Kleinknecht, H., 115, 123
Koester, H., 8, 16, 28, 32, 33, 34, 35, 36, 111
Kümmel, W. G., 64
LaGrange, R. P. M., 136
Lane, W., 1, 36, 37, 78, 105, 116
Liefeld, W. L., 102
Lindars, B., 89
Loader, W. R. G., 73
Lohse, E., 67
Longenecker, R., 64, 75, 92, 124
Lucian of Samosata, 34, 104
Luz, U., 27
Markan Christology, 1, 23, 25, 26, 27, 28, 29, 30, 31, 33, 35, 37, 70, 71, 99, 126, 127, 130, 132, 133
Marshall, I. H., 66, 68, 78, 83, 92, 110, 124
von Martitz, P. W., 100, 101, 124
Martyn, J. L., 69
martyr, 18, 101
Mauser, U., 128
McCarthy, D., 46
McDermott, J., 66, 82, 93
Mercer, S. A. B., 51
Messiah/messiahship, 11, 15, 22, 29, 37, 39, 49, 50, 59, 63, 64, 65, 66, 67, 68, 69, 70, 71, 73, 74,

75, 76, 77, 78, 79, 83, 84, 85, 87,
  88, 91, 93, 94, 95, 96, 127, 128,
  129, 133, 140, 141
Miller, J. M., 56
miracle-worker, 1, 2, 12, 24, 26,
  31, 70, 133, 136
miracle-working, 3, 18, 19, 31,
  106, 109, 118, 119, 128, 132, 133,
Moody, D., 83
Moses, 26, 28, 35, 38, 45, 48, 67,
  69, 88, 109, 110, 111, 117, 127,
  133
Moule, C. F. D., 64, 82, 85
Mowinckel, S., 51, 57
mystery religions, 10, 11, 126
Nicol, W., 12, 112, 113, 131
Nock, A. D., 9, 119, 130, 131, 136
Nolan, B., 74, 76, 79, 86
Noth, M., 50
O'Connell, M., 47
Ogden, S., 21, 22
Payne, J. B., 88
Perrin, N., 31
Philo, 10, 14, 21, 28, 36, 38, 108,
  109, 110, 114, 115, 117, 119, 122,
  124
Philostratus, 36, 104, 118
Plato, 16, 17, 103, 115, 118, 131,
  140
Prümm, K., 106
Pythagoras, 15, 28, 100, 104, 131,
  140
Qumran, 64, 65, 66, 67, 86, 108,
  127
von Rad, G., 53, 55, 74, 113
Reitzenstein, R., 10, 12, 24, 35
religionsgeschichte, 8, 9
resurrection, 65, 66, 68, 69, 91, 93
Robinson, J., 32, 33
Roth, W., 56, 74
van Ruler, A., 76, 86
Sabourin, L., 58, 69, 137

Schmithals, W., 111
Schniewind, J., 74, 141
Schreiber, J., 25, 27
Schweizer, E., 84, 103
shalom, 73, 74, 75, 76
"signs source," 30, 35
Smith, M., 28, 99, 102, 115, 125
Son of David, 67, 71, 72, 73, 74,
  76, 77, 91, 128
Son of God, 1, 2, 3, 5, 10, 11, 12,
  13, 15, 19, 22, 23, 24, 25, 26, 28,
  30, 31, 33, 37, 38, 39, 63, 64, 65,
  66, 67, 68, 70, 71, 73, 74, 75, 77,
  78, 79, 80, 81, 82, 83, 85, 86, 87,
  89, 90, 91, 92, 93, 94, 95, 96, 97,
  99, 120, 121, 123, 124, 125, 126,
  129, 130, 132, 136, 137
Strack-Billerbeck, 80
Taylor, V., 77, 90
theios, 15, 17, 25, 32, 97, 100, 101,
  102, 103, 105, 109, 112, 119, 132,
  136, 139
theios anēr, 1, 2, 3, 7, 9, 10, 12,
  15, 17, 18, 19, 20, 22, 23, 24, 25,
  26, 27, 28, 29, 30, 31, 32, 33, 36,
  37, 38, 97, 99, 100, 101, 102, 104,
  105, 107, 109, 110, 112, 113, 114,
  116, 118, 119, 120, 123, 129, 130,
  131, 132
θεῖος, 9, 11, 12, 13, 17, 18, 19, 23,
  24, 101, 102, 110, 119, 121, 123,
  128, 130, 132, 133, 139, 140, 141
"theology of glory," 25, 27, 28, 29
"theology of the cross," 25, 27
Thompson, J. A., 81
Tiede, D. L., 100, 101, 103, 104,
  106, 109, 121, 131
"transference theory," 9, 21, 24,
  38, 63
de Vaux, R., 52, 53, 58
Vermes, G., 72, 73, 89
Vielhauer, P., 27

Vriezen, Th. C., 48
Weeden, T., 28, 29, 31, 99
Weinfeld, M., 46
Weinreich, O., 13, 14, 139
Weiser, A., 53, 54
Weiss, J., 8
Wetter, G., 11, 12, 13, 99, 103,
    106, 124, 139
Wilder, A., 112
Williamson, L., 79
Windisch, H., 14, 15, 139
Wrede, W., 71
Young, F., 32
Youngblood, R., 88